The Shadow Puppet Book

The Shadow Puppet Book

Janet Lynch-Watson

Sterling Publishing Co., Inc.   New York

Oak Tree Press Co., Ltd.
London & Sydney

Dedication
To M. L. M.

Acknowledgments

I would like to thank all those whose help and encouragement have made this book possible. I am particularly grateful to my team of puppeteers, Angini, Frances, Lynn, Robin, Rowena, Sam and Wai-Fong.

My thanks are due to Olive Blackham for permission to use material from her book *Shadow Puppets* (Barrie & Rockcliff 1960) and to Sylvia K. Shiel for allowing me to reproduce her illustration of Hsia K'e in *Shadow Puppets*. My thanks also to Hetta Empson to whom the puppet, Hsia K'e, belongs.

I am indebted to John Anderson who took the photographs and to Anne Grimwade for her assistance with musical settings.

Finally I would like to thank Sheila Barry for invaluable professional advice and patient encouragement throughout the production of this book.

Photo of Prince Panji on page 126 courtesy of the British Museum.

Second Printing, 1980

Copyright © 1980 by Janet Lynch-Watson
Published by Sterling Publishing Co., Inc.
Two Park Avenue, New York, N.Y. 10016
Distributed in Australia by Oak Tree Press Co., Ltd.,
P.O. Box J34, Brickfield Hill, Sydney 2000, N.S.W.
Distributed in the United Kingdom by Ward Lock Ltd.
116 Baker Street, London W.1
Manufactured in the United States of America
All rights reserved
Library of Congress Catalog Card No.: 79-65069
Sterling ISBN 0-8069-7030-8 Trade   Oak Tree 7061-2665-3
0-8069-7031-6 Library

CONTENTS

Illus. 1. A shadow puppet play in production.
A shadow puppet theatre can be put together from a few strips of wood, a piece of fabric and a light. Puppets are easy and quick to make. In this theatre, a Chinese-type dragon play is in rehearsal. Lynn is operating the dragon, while Robin works the wizard. Angini is getting ready for her puppet's appearance. Sam is in charge of the lighting. See page 32 for the audience view of this scene.

1. What's It All About?

Have you ever seen an animal like this—a shadow figure on a wall? You've probably made one yourself. With the right lighting, it's easy enough: you simply move your hands and fingers into different positions and there, on the wall, is cast a shadow.

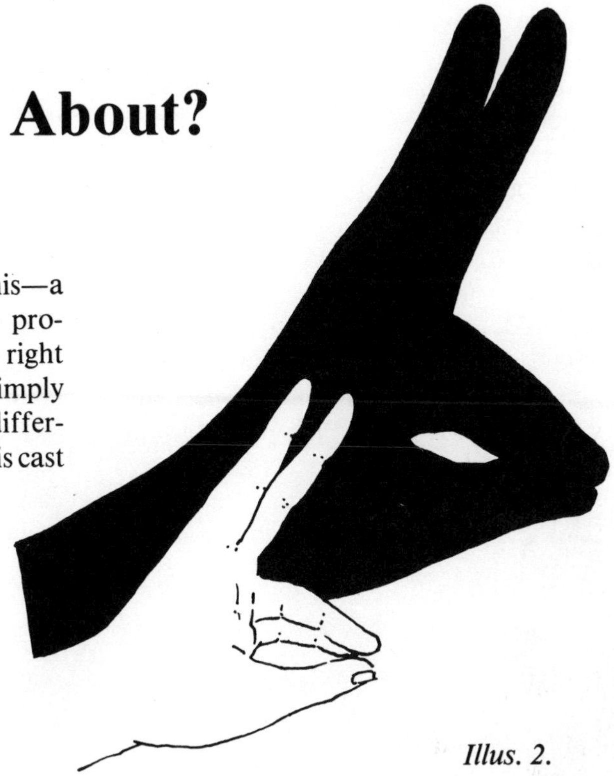

Illus. 2.

Shadow puppets work in much the same way, but instead of your hands, you use flat puppets. You can see how it works in the photograph on the opposite page. Facing the audience is a screen made of thin white paper or fabric. It is stretched tightly over a frame. A few feet (metres) behind this screen, on the side away from the audience, is a bright light. All other lights are turned off. Between the screen and the light, pressed hard against the screen, flat figures—usually made of cardboard—are controlled by rods.

What exactly does the audience see? It sees silhouette figures moving across a screen. These may be simple black shapes, or they may be decorated in some way and gleam with color. Provided that you hold them flat against the screen, with strong light behind them, their outlines appear strong and distinct. The effect is similar to that of a sharp shadow.

Ordinary string or glove puppets are viewed directly by the audience. Shadow puppets are not; they are separated from the audience by the screen. They rely on the light not only to produce the image seen by the audience, but also to transform them from rather shabby pieces of cardboard into characters of magic and beauty.

Although other types of puppets, particularly string and glove puppets, have become popular in recent years, shadow puppets have been neglected. This is a pity, because this branch of puppetry offers great scope, not only to beginners, but also to those who seek more elaborate effects.

In this book you'll find out how to make a shadow puppet screen and fix up a light, create various types of puppets, and give your own shadow puppet entertainments. Colored cardboard and paper, tinted cellophane*, acetate sheet, tissue paper, polyethylene (soft plastic), lace, fabric scraps, wrapping paper,

pressed flowers and leaves—you can use all these materials to give variety to your shadow puppets and shadow theatre scenery.

When your screen is ready and your puppets prepared, you will be able to entertain your family and friends from a vast range of material waiting to be adapted for the shadow theatre. Ballet, folktales, music, poetry and drama can all provide ideas for shadow puppet performances to suit the abilities and inventiveness of people of all ages. You can call upon a cast that includes gods and goddesses, all sorts of monsters, historical characters, famous personalities, or even your top television or cartoon characters. The possibilities are endless.

*Cellophane in England is a trade-mark belonging to British Cellophane Ltd.

2. The Staging

The materials for making a puppet theatre are neither expensive nor hard to find. You can probably improvise with materials you already have around the house, if you're planning just one puppet entertainment. If you decide to do more, it's easy to make more permanent equipment, and you can make it to suit your own needs.

Three things are essential:

- a screen
- a light
- puppets

The Picture Frame Screen

This is a wooden frame with thin fabric, usually cotton, stretched tightly over it. You can use a large picture frame, if you want. If you're going to construct the frame yourself, though, make it on the large side—somewhere between 28-40 inches (70-100 cm) for the short vertical sides and between 42-60 inches (105-150 cm) for the long horizontal sides. This gives you more scope for using your puppets.

To build the frame, use pieces of wood (called battens) that measure approximately 1½ inches wide by ½ inch thick (4 cm by 1½ cm). Cut the two long pieces and the two short pieces. Place them flat on the floor in a rectangle and join them together by nailing triangles of Masonite (hardboard) to the corners. Four pieces

of Masonite (hardboard) 6 inches square (15 cm) and cut diagonally will give you eight triangles. Use one on each side of each corner to keep the frame rigid.

While most screens are made of fabric, thin paper will also work, but it tears easily, and you may need to replace it from time to time. In productions that call for the same scenery throughout, using paper, you can paint the scene right onto the screen itself. Then you don't need to set up scenery at all, and there is

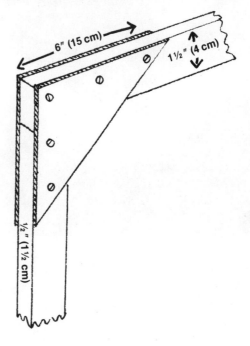

Illus. 3. Corner of frame strengthened with Masonite (hardboard) triangle.

9

Illus. 4. Wai-Fong, Rowena and Sam are tacking fabric to a frame to make the shadow screen. Sam is using a staple gun, but he could just as easily use a hammer and tacks. Rowena is pulling the material taut.

less equipment to get in the way of the puppets. For plays like these, a paper screen is preferable.

Whatever material you use for the screen—paper or cotton—it is important to stretch it and tack it very tightly to the frame. Creases or slackness distort the shadows. You can attach a paper screen to the frame with transparent tape or tacks. With a fabric screen, use small carpet tacks or a staple gun.

Supporting the Screen

To get shadows with sharp outlines, you'll be holding your puppets close to the screen, so you must be sure that your screen is firm and won't wobble. You can do this in various ways. Take another look at the illustration on page 6. The most comfortable way to operate the puppets is in a kneeling or standing position. The screen needs to be above your head, so that you don't cast a shadow on the screen and shield the puppets from the operating light.

One way to keep the frame secure is with clamps, the sort carpenters use to keep their work in position. This is a good method, if you can find a piece of furniture on which to rest the screen—a table, for example, as shown in the illustration on page 6. To protect the table from screw marks, insert pieces of cardboard between clamp and table. With this system, you keep your equipment to a minimum. A flat screen is easy to store.

The Folding Screen Theatre

You can convert an old-fashioned folding screen into a permanent shadow puppet screen or adapt it for a single performance.

The upper section of the middle panel forms the actual screen. The sides fold back at an angle towards the puppeteers and keep the screen upright. You need to cover them—and the bottom section of the middle panel—with an opaque material to hide you from the audience.

Illus. 5. A shadow puppet screen made from an old-fashioned folding screen.

Other Screens

There are other ways to construct a screen. A doorway with paper stretched across it will work quite well, and you may get other ideas. Whatever you use, make sure the screen is firm, and leave plenty of room behind it for the light and the puppeteers.

The Working Shelf

No matter what kind of screen you use, a working shelf, set about 6-8 inches (15-20 cm) below the bottom of the screen, is a good place to prop up the rods of the puppets when the puppeteers are busy elsewhere. Cover it with foam rubber, a towel, or some other crumpled material.

Testing

When you start work on your puppets and scenery, it helps enormously to test the effects as you go along. For instance, you may want to find out how much light shines through a piece of fabric, or whether the outline you've cut for a puppet is distinct. Rather than set up the screen every time, it's very convenient to have a smaller screen handy which you can hold up to the light. A medium-sized picture frame, covered with thin white paper, is invaluable for this purpose.

The Light

Again, you may be able to improvise. The light should point towards the screen. If it is so bright that you can see the actual bulb through the screen, you

may have to beam it from above the screen or from one side. You can use a modern standing lamp with an adjustable angled bulb, as in the illustration on page 6. A slide projector is also satisfactory.

If you use an ordinary table lamp, you have to place it on its side in order to point it towards the screen. To keep it steady, find a large, sturdy cardboard tube, such as those used inside rolls of carpet, approximately 6-8 inches (15-20 cm) in diameter. Cut it down to size: a tube more than 2 feet (60 cm) high will be unsteady. Cut a groove into the top of the tube and place the neck of the lamp in it.

Illus. 6. Table lamp used as an operating lamp. Notice that the lamp shade has been turned upside down so that it will throw the light forward.

Illus. 7. Sam and Wai-Fong test a puppet for "The Owl and the Pussy-Cat" on a small picture frame screen which they hold up to the light.

You can, of course, make your own light by buying all the component parts—bulb, lightholder, electric cord, and plug—and attach them to a stand.

Whatever method you use, remember that all electrical appliances should be treated with care. An electric light bulb can become very hot. Make sure your arrangement is safe and not likely to cause a fire.

If it is not possible for you to create artificial light, don't give up. Often natural light, coming through a window, is enough to illuminate the screen, especially if you can darken other windows in the room.

Scenery

It is not always necessary to use scenery, but it provides an effective background for your puppets. The type of scenery, of course, depends on the entertainment you are putting on. You'll find specific ideas for sets later in the notes on each play. The bottom of the frame provides a natural straight "floor" for your puppets, but you may want to vary that and show long grass, for example, or a slope. If you do, you need to make a "ground piece." This is simply a horizontal strip of cardboard which you place along the base of the screen. It is shaped to represent a slope, or grass, or whatever. It also helps to raise the action nearer the middle of the screen.

The best way to attach the ground piece is to insert it between the frame and the screen. If you can't do that, try nailing a cardboard flap along the bottom batten of the screen.

Attach taller pieces near the top with a pin, a stitch, or a soft, sticky modelling material, such as plasticine, or transparent tape.

Good scenery can provide an impressive background for the puppets and it's worth taking trouble over it. You can work on the scenery beforehand, of course, so that you don't need to bother with it during the actual performance.

Cardboard comes in different colors, and you can use it to vary your effects. Even dark-colored cardboard shows up on the screen, if the operating light is strong. Pink cardboard glows most attractively; it is ideal for a turreted fairy tale castle.

Colored tissue paper or, if you can afford it, colored acetate sheet, gives a

Illus. 8. This ground piece, with tree, was cut from one piece of cardboard. The leaf area of the tree is backed with green tissue paper, so that the cut-out leaves give a green glow. The ground piece will need to be fastened to the screen with a pin, with soft modelling material such as plasticine, a stitch, or with transparent tape.

sense of depth to shadow scenery. Try overlapping different colors, cutting out patterns and shapes, or painting the tissue paper. The effects are exciting.

If you create scenery from paper or thin cardboard, you can give it detail with felt pens or paint. The house shown below is made from brown paper. The roof has been painted dark grey to suggest slates, and the tiles and bricks have been outlined with a felt pen. The brown paper gives a warm, textured glow on the screen.

Illus. 9. This house, made of paper, won't stand up against the screen by itself, so you need to attach it firmly with a pin. Putting transparent tape over the windows is another way to keep your house in place on the screen, but if the screen is made of paper, it's liable to tear when you remove the house.

To sum up: there are several ways you can dress up a piece of scenery:

- by using colored cardboard
- by cutting away parts of the scenery and backing these cutaway parts with tissue paper or acetate sheet in a contrasting color
- by adding decorations to that backing
- by using paper or cardboard thin enough to reveal details you add with felt pen or paint.

Cardboard and paper are not the only materials suitable for scenery. You can use almost anything that is flat enough. Flowers, leaves, and grasses add a realistic touch, but press them first (more about this on page 39). Even household discards can be effective. For instance, you can make the hunter's net in the play "The Lion and the Mouse" (see page 78) from a net vegetable bag.

Another scenery technique is to paint the scene onto a sheet of tissue paper the same size as the screen. You'll find more about this method in the stage directions for "The Lion and the Mouse" (see page 85).

Of course, if you use a slide projector as an operating light, it is possible to project scenery onto your screen. You need to have an appropriate photographic slide, or you could paint the scene on a plain glass slide. Art and hobby shops sell glass-painting colors which you can use for this purpose. A photographic slide can be an impressive backdrop, but it is not always easy to find one that is the right scale for the puppets and which, because of its detail, doesn't detract from them.

When you design scenery for your puppets, it is important not to clutter the screen with too many objects. Use only what is necessary to the action and leave your puppets plenty of room to move about on the screen.

A Table Shadow Theatre

The larger your screen, the greater scope you will have for your shadow productions. However, screen, lights and puppets all take up storage space which you may not be able to spare. The answer to this space problem may be a table shadow theatre.

You'll need a strong cardboard carton. Stand it up on one of its small sides and cut out one half of the base to make a space for a screen leaving about an inch (2½ cm) border.

Draw a line around three sides of the carton, dividing each side in half. Cut away the top end and bend back the two sides. This will give you more operating space, and the sides will form convenient "wings" to mask the puppeteers. You can strengthen the whole structure by nailing battens (strips) of wood inside. Use white fabric or paper for your screen. A flashlight (torch) or a lantern (bicycle lamp) is good for an operating light. Be sure to use new batteries to give a bright beam, but remove the reflector to prevent the light from focussing on one particular spot.

To improve the appearance of the theatre, cover it with wallpaper, wrapping paper, or adhesive paper. You can operate it comfortably by sitting behind it at a table.

When you give a performance in your table shadow theatre, you will be limited to just one puppeteer, but there is still a great deal within your scope.

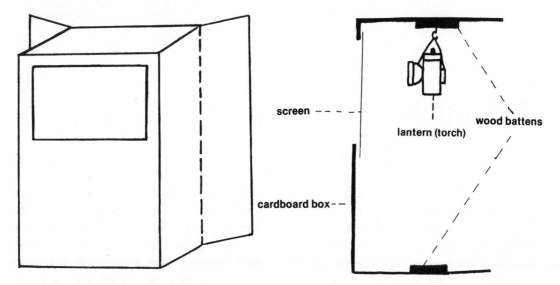

Illus. 10. Cardboard box with screen cut out and sides bent back.

Illus. 11. Cross-section of box showing position of light.

screen

lantern (torch)

wood battens

cardboard box

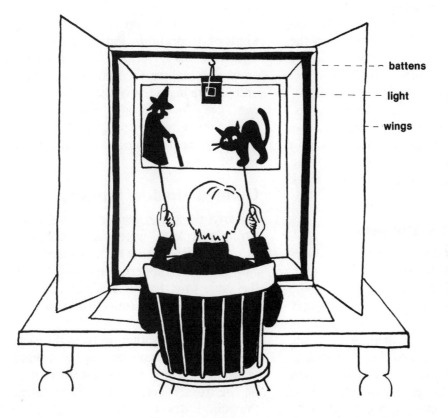

battens

light

wings

Naturally, the puppets for a table theatre need to be smaller than those for a larger screen. In every other respect, though, you can follow the suggestions in this book for making puppets and scenery.

Illus. 12. Table shadow theatre in operation.

3. Puppets

How big should shadow puppets be? This depends on the size of your screen. As a very rough guide, an average human figure should be about one-third the height of the screen. The type of action dictates the size in some cases. For instance, a play with many very active characters would call for smaller puppets than a performance with a few characters with limited movements. A "head and shoulders" puppet, such as the one on page 42, would be much larger than the whole body of one of the puppets in the play "The Emperor's New Clothes."

Shadow puppets have been made of many different materials. Animal skins, wood, wire, sheet tin and cardboard are just a few of them. For our purposes, thin cardboard is the most practical. It should be thin enough to cut easily, but thick enough to stay rigid.

Black Shadow Puppets

Very dark or thick cardboard produces a black shadow. It blocks out all the light. Although such puppets are simple, the black figures on a white screen can be very dramatic.

You can decorate them with tissue paper, fabric scraps, or almost anything. The laughing girl on page 19 has a dotted blouse. The dots were cut out with a hole puncher and backed with colored tissue paper or thin fabric. She is wearing a white apron. Here, the cardboard was cut away and replaced with white paper. The dragon puppet on page 31 is made from a grocery carton. Two panels are cut away and replaced with a piece of clear self-adhesive vinyl, decorated with a tissue paper pattern. Eyes, nostril and a tongue of fire are made of red tissue paper. The dragon's wings are edged with green paper.

Use your imagination to find other kinds of decorations. Paper cake doilies, scraps of lace, loosely woven fabric, embossed wallpaper, thin foam rubber and foil are just a few of the materials you can use for exciting effects. It is important, however, to keep the puppet firm. If you cut too much away, the figure will be weak.

Colored Shadow Puppets

Early puppets, such as those from China and Java, were made of beaten skins to which color was then added. We can paint our modern puppets in much the same way. In this case, it is best to make the figures from firm white or pastel cardboard.

We can take another tip from the early Eastern puppets and use oil for a more translucent effect. First paint the puppet on the front "screen" side. Then, when the paint is dry, apply a coating of oil to the back "rod" side of the puppet. You can use almost any clear oil, but artists' refined linseed oil is particularly good. You may need to thin it with turpentine before using it, since the best consistency is that of ordinary vegetable oil. Leave the puppet to absorb the oil and dry out until it no longer feels sticky. This usually takes up to two days.

Silhouette Puppets

Shadow puppets can be simple or very complicated. It's surprising how effective a plain silhouette – with no jointed parts – can be. When you design such a character, decide first whether it needs to face front or to be in profile. If you use it in profile, determine which side you want the figure to face. It is possible to use the same figure facing left and right, but it can be tricky. You need either a very thin rod – or a removable rod which you can fix easily to either side of the puppet – or a cardboard rod which is a continuation of the puppet. The cardboard rod method is used for the hen puppet on page 72.

When you sketch the puppet, use the outline to tell the audience as much as you can about the character. This is important in the design of all shadow puppets, but especially for simple silhouettes.

Illus. 13. The figure at the left has very little personality. It is lifeless and stiff. Compare it with the old man and laughing girl. Each has an outline that reveals character.

Attaching the Operating Rod

You can manipulate the puppets with rods made of wire or wood. Wire coat hangers, thin garden rods and thick basketwork canes all work well. Best of all are the bundles of very thin rigid wires that are sold in craft shops. In the picture of the Chinese puppet on page 127 the wire rods are pushed into lengths of bamboo cane. This is a good idea which you may want to copy: the bamboo handle is comfortable to hold, and at the same time, the wire part makes only a very faint shadow on the screen. Whatever sort of rod you choose, it must be rigid enough to hold the puppet flat against the screen.

When the rod you use is thin enough, you can operate the puppet facing either right or left. Just turn the puppet around to face the other way. A very thin wire rod won't keep the puppet too far away from the screen and it won't show when it's between the puppet and the screen.

There are several ways to attach rods. If you're working very close to the screen — standing rather than kneeling — you can tape the rod flat against the puppet. When you work close to the screen, though, you don't have room for a shelf to prop the rods on, and this is a drawback.

It's usually easier to work the puppets if you stand a little distance away from them. Then you can use a hinged attachment. The rod used for the second dog (right) is attached by a hinge made from transparent tape. There are many ways to make a hinge. The wire and paper fasteners used to close plastic food bags can be bent easily and taped to the rod and the puppet.

You can make another type of hinge from a small piece of cardboard — about ½ inch by 2½ inches (1½ cm by 6 cm) — folded across the middle and taped to the rod and puppet.

Illus. 14. Flat rod attachment.

Illus. 15. Hinged attachment.

20

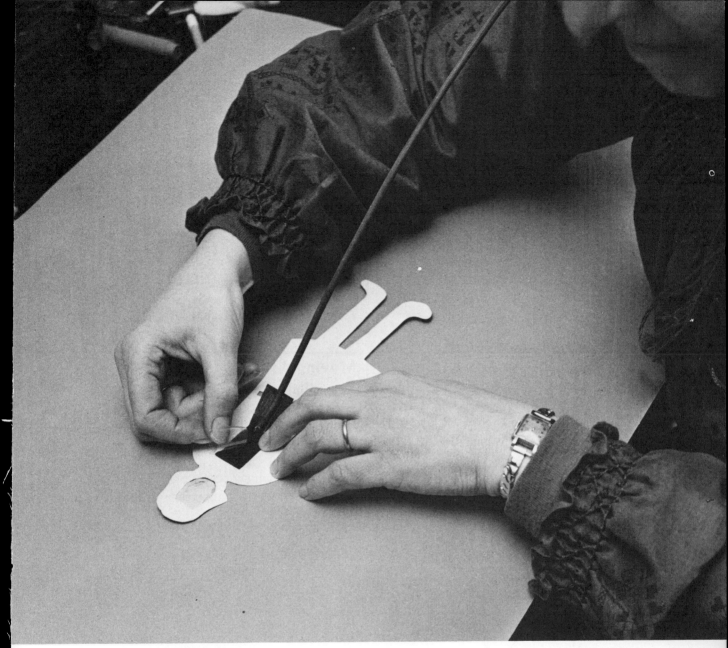

Illus. 16.

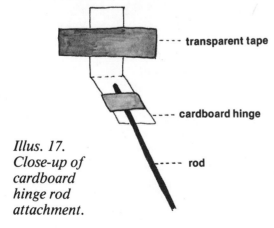

- - - - transparent tape

- - - - cardboard hinge

- - - - rod

*Illus. 17.
Close-up of
cardboard
hinge rod
attachment.*

With these hinged methods, your puppet can be stored flat.

Some puppeteers prefer to have a limited number of rods which they attach to a puppet when needed. This system has the advantage that the rods can be cut to exactly the right length for your particular theatre, so that when the puppets are propped up, with the rods resting on the working shelf, they are in the right

21

part of the screen. To create these detachable rods, punch a staple into the puppet. Then you just ease the bent rod under the staple. It is important that the wire rod is held firmly in place by the staple.

If you're going to do only one puppet play, you're probably better off using the regular fixed rods. If you do several plays, detachable rods may be more convenient – it will be easier to store the puppets and you need fewer rods.

Making Puppets Move

Although simple silhouette figures are effective, you'll surely want to try more complex figures. The action of your puppet play may call upon the characters to do some specific movements. Moving sections need more rods, and this complicates the puppeteer's job.

Most people find it easy to operate two rods at a time. Operating three rods is sometimes possible. More than three is difficult – too difficult for most people to manage. You can, of course, link two moving parts to one rod, if you're willing to have them move together all the time. The hen on page 72 is a good example.

Moving Arms and Legs

Sometimes it's effective to have an arm or leg divided into separate joints, with a rod on just one of them. Look at the arms on the Chinese and Javanese puppets on pages 126 and 127. They were designed this way to achieve natural movement without making the puppeteer's task too difficult.

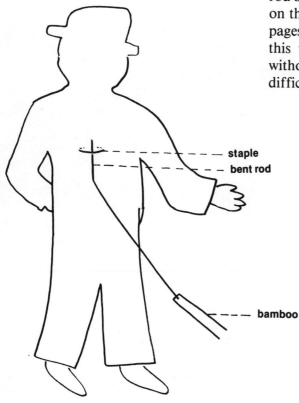

— staple

— bent rod

— bamboo

Illus. 18. Detachable rod kept in place by staple. It's important that the wire rod is held firmly in place by the staple.

Illus. 19. Ballet Dancer.
The left arm of this dancer is jointed, with a rod on only one section. Both of her legs are jointed at the hip, but only her left leg has an operating rod. Her right leg moves freely. So does her right arm, which is jointed at the elbow. This puppet is unusual in that it has no rod attached to its body. Firm control is provided by the arm and leg rods alone.

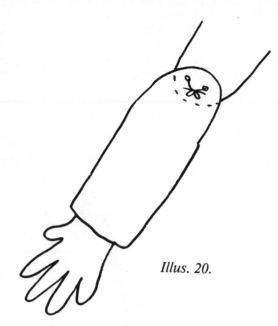

Illus. 20.

overlapping sections

thread, loosely joining overlay

Illus. 21.

The edges where joints overlap should be gently rounded to avoid jutting corners and stilted movement. Small paper fasteners give a firm join, but sometimes you'll want to get fluid movement, as in the case of the Ballet Dancer, where strong thread was used.

You can get other parts of your puppet to move, too, not only arms and legs.

Your puppet can be jointed at the waist, for example, allowing it to bend. A jointed chin piece can give the impression of speech. Animals' tails can wag and their ears can droop. The dragon which you see in some of the photographs is made in four separate sections; this gives a good range of movement.

paper fastener

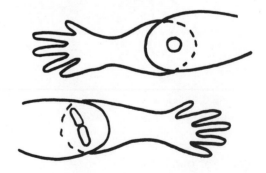

Illus. 22. Cross section showing two sections joined by a paper fastener.

Illus. 23. An arm in two sections, joined by a paper fastener. This diagram shows both back and front.

24

Sometimes you will want to stop a jointed section from moving beyond a certain point. For instance, if the Ballet Dancer's left leg rises above the side of her dress, it will destroy the illusion. You can prevent this by linking the leg and dress sections with a piece of thread – or you can stick a strip of cardboard along the edge of her skirt – so that her leg can't move past it. As you rehearse with your puppets, you'll find similar problems arising, and you can adapt these tricks to solve them.

Fabric Parts

Another way to achieve movement in a puppet is to substitute fabric – or even thick rope – for a part of the puppet's body. An arm or leg made of fabric allows for some elaborate actions. It is important, however, to match the fabric to the material the puppet is made from, both in color and the degree to which light shines through it. Then no one will notice the change from cardboard to fabric. Dark felt is a good fabric to use, because light does not penetrate it. When you work with such a puppet, be careful not to exaggerate its movements, or the realistic effect will be lost.

Real People Puppets and Caricatures

If you ever stood in the light of a slide or film projector, you know that a very distinct shadow of yourself appeared on the screen. From such a shadow outline, you can create puppets of people you know.

This is how it's done. Rule a large sheet

of white paper with squares about 4 inches by 4 inches (10 cm by 10 cm). Ask your subjects to stand beside it, a few inches (centimetres) away, facing sideways. Shine a strong light at them and ask them to keep as still as possible while you quickly trace around their outlines. If you have a projector handy, use that. The shadows it casts are very sharp.

Now, on small pieces of cardboard, rule squares 1¼ inches by 1¼ inches (3 cm by 3 cm). Scale down your shadow profiles to this size. Now you have outlined heads from which to make the puppets. You can make an outline for the whole body in the same way , but generally it isn't necessary. This technique works best with people who have distinctive profiles.

You can also use profile photographs to get an outline of a person. Ask your subject to stand in front of a sheet of white paper when you take the photograph. In this case, you need to scale *up* the outline you get from the print.

Magazine photographs can provide wonderful two-dimensional outlines. You can use them as a guide when you make puppets in action, such as football players or galloping horses. They can also help when you need to create figures in special costumes, like firemen, African tribal dancers, or Eskimos. You may not be able to use a direct tracing of the figure for your puppet, but the outlines give valuable information about important features.

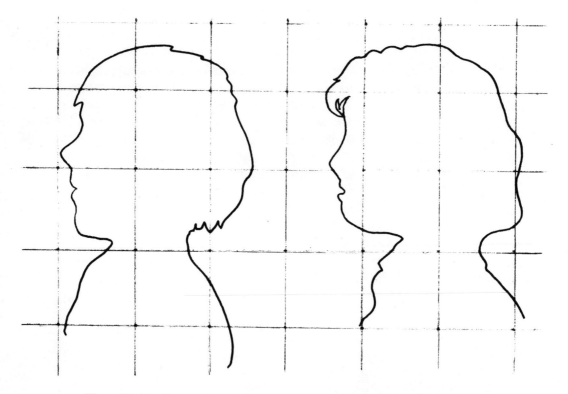

Illus. 25. Outlines of shadow profiles scaled down to puppet size.

Group Puppets

Suppose you want to produce a play which has a group of characters who always appear together—perhaps five fierce wolves or a dozen Keystone Kops, a line of soldiers, a host of angels, or a swarm of bees—don't be put off by the number! Providing that they always appear together and that none of them has an individual action to perform, make them as one puppet—a group puppet—so that they can all be operated by one person.

Illus. 26. Red tissue paper behind the cut-out eyes and red tissue paper tongues give a fierce appearance to these wolves, cut from dark cardboard.

Chinese-type Puppets

In China, shadow puppetry flourished for many centuries. Chinese shadow puppets were ornate and particularly durable, since they were made of treated animal skins. The ones we see in museums are evidence of the respect the Chinese gave to the art, no doubt because the plays were an excellent way to teach about Chinese history and the Buddhist faith. More about the history of these puppets on page 125. Meanwhile, we can learn a great deal from the Chinese techniques. If you want to make a more sophisticated and elaborately decorated puppet than any described so far, try the following design, based loosely on a Chinese figure.

Its body and head are combined in one piece. It has two leg sections and two arms—each with two joints—seven pieces in all.

The figure is made from two thicknesses of white cardboard glued together. The two layers give strength, and you can sandwich between them a thin decorated layer.

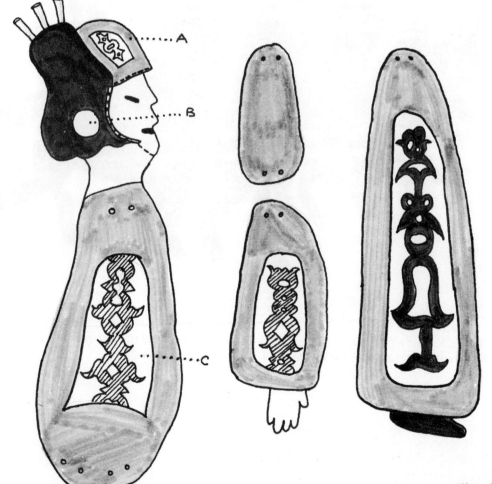

Illus. 27.

28

The body piece

You'll see that the face area (forehead to chin) in the puppet on page 28 is marked by white dotted lines in the illustration. On *one layer only,* this area is completely cut away. The light can penetrate the remaining layer more brightly than if there were two layers, allowing the mouth and eye to stand out clearly.

First color the puppet with a felt pen, leaving the face and neck white. Use black for the hair and another color for the rest. Remove the three pieces marked A, B and C altogether. Then paint the whole piece with thinned linseed oil (see page 18) to give it a translucent appearance. Glue a piece of red fabric to the inside of one layer over circle B.

To decorate the helmet and jacket, use tissue paper cut-outs. Elaborate papercutting is a Chinese craft (appropriate to use here). Take two shades of tissue paper, one light in color and one dark. Use the light tissue for a background and cut pieces of both just a little larger than the holes you have to fill (A and C). You create the decorative pattern in the dark tissue by folding it, and then cutting the folded paper (paper-doll fashion) and opening it out. It's easy to do and very effective, but practice on scraps of tissue paper first.

Now take a piece of clear self-adhesive vinyl (you can buy it in rolls; it's sometimes sold for covering books) about the same size as the tissue sheet. Peel off the backing. Place the cut-out piece of tissue on the sticky side of the vinyl, and follow it with the light background piece of tissue. This triple sandwich is then placed between the two body layers, which can now be glued together. Finally, decorate the helmet with three short lengths cut from a striped drinking straw.

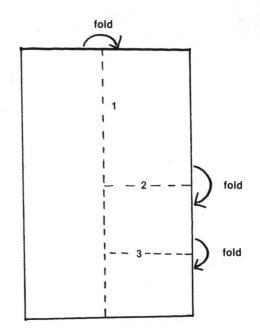

Illus. 28. Tissue paper to be folded 3 times.

Illus. 29. Shaded parts cut away from folded paper.

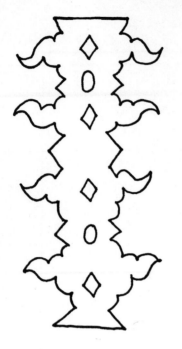

Illus. 30. Unfolded tissue pattern.

The arms and legs

You make the arms in the same way as the body piece, with two layers of cardboard, painted and oiled, sandwiching in a decorated tissue paper design.

The legs are patterned in a different way. Remove the central panel from only *one* of the leg pieces. Draw a black felt pen decoration on the other layer before you paint it with oil. If you wish, you can use the same form of decoration for both arms and legs. The wizard in the Chinese dragon story shown on the front cover is made in a similar way to the Chinese shadow puppet but has no moving parts.

Moving sections and rods

The separate sections of the puppet are loosely connected with strong thread. Small pinprick holes in the illustration on page 28 indicate the points where the connections are made. Attaching the rod at the neck of the puppet, as in the illustration below, makes it possible to use the puppet facing both ways.

If you make this type of puppet, keep in mind that the number of moving parts —and the positions of the rods—need to be determined by the actions the puppet has to perform.

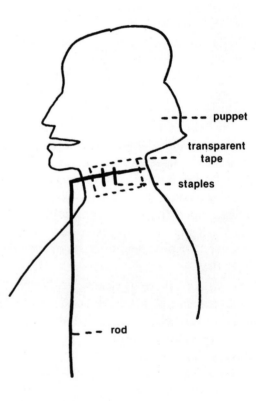
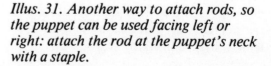

Illus. 31. Another way to attach rods, so the puppet can be used facing left or right: attach the rod at the puppet's neck with a staple.

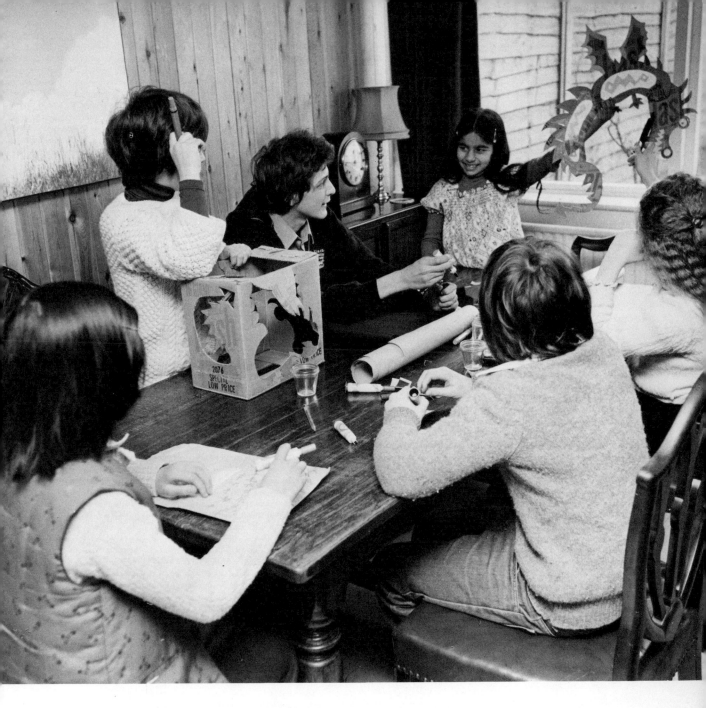

Illus. 32. Angini holds up a completed dragon puppet for the others to admire. Rowena has the grocery carton from which it was cut. The puppet was made in four parts, loosely joined with strong thread.

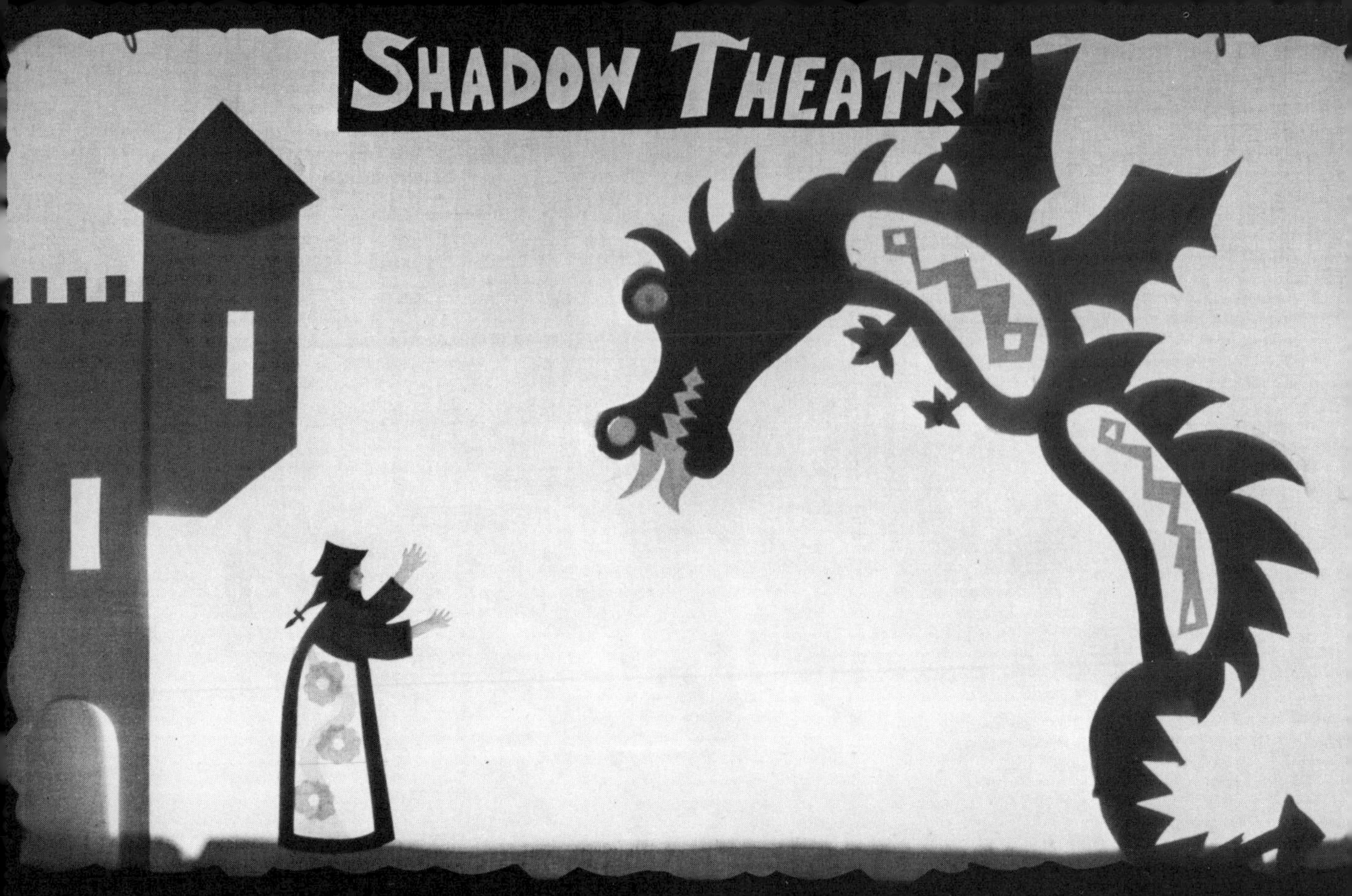
SHADOW THEATR

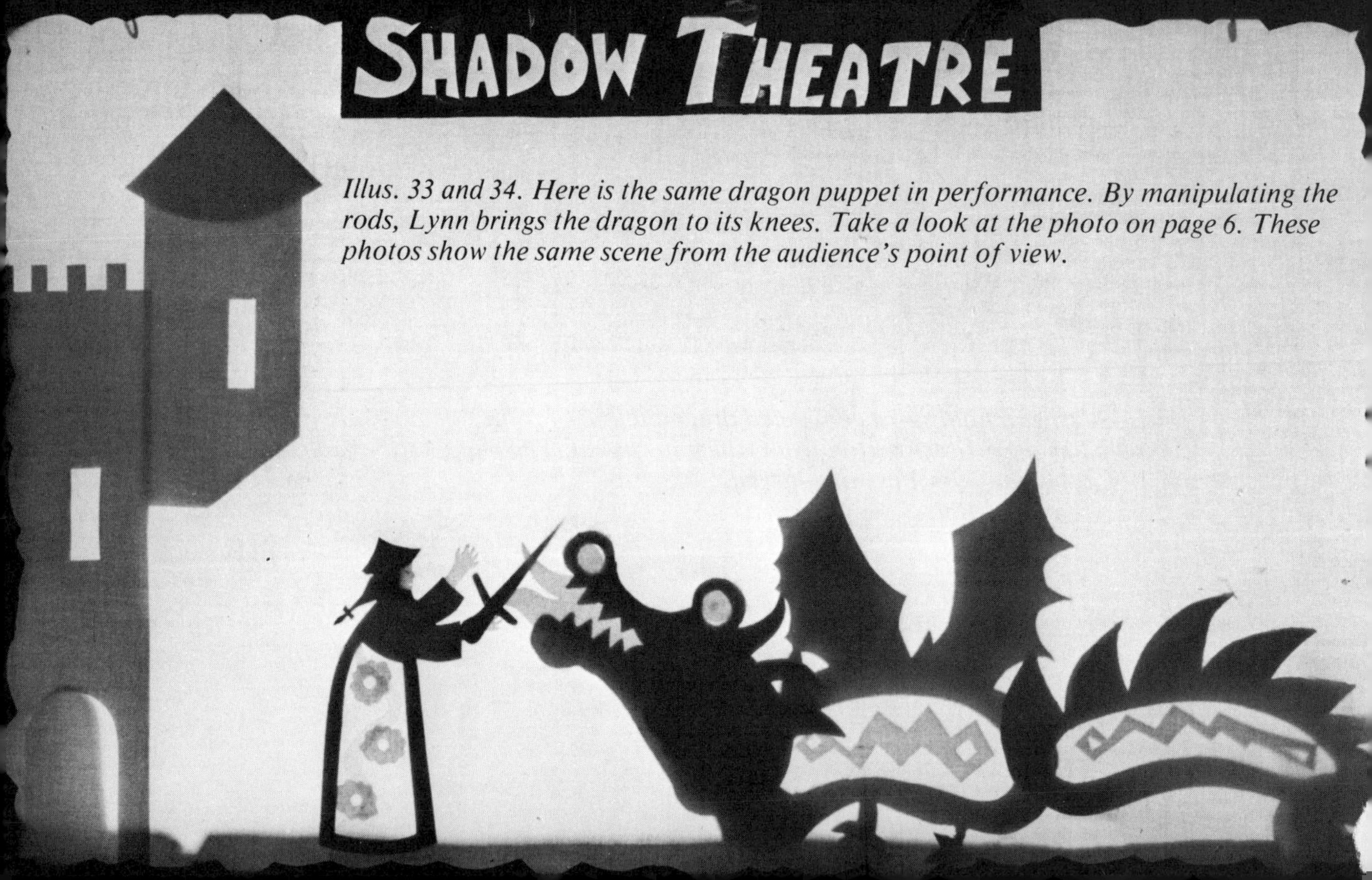
SHADOW THEATRE

Illus. 33 and 34. Here is the same dragon puppet in performance. By manipulating the rods, Lynn brings the dragon to its knees. Take a look at the photo on page 6. These photos show the same scene from the audience's point of view.

Unusual Puppets

So far, all the puppets have been made in a fairly conventional way. There is, however, plenty of room for experiment. Perhaps the actions you want from a puppet will suggest new ideas for you to try. Sometimes the character of the puppet demands that it be created in a different way! Here are three examples of puppets which are designed very differently from the cardboard figures.

A Ghost

You make this puppet from thin soft fabric. Use any material that falls naturally into folds. Its color doesn't really matter, providing that light shines through it to give the ghost a misty look. Grey nylon jersey is excellent. If you made the little screen from a picture frame (see page 13), you'll find it easy to try out different materials such as muslin, greaseproof paper, polyethylene (soft plastic), cotton or whatever, until you achieve the effect you want.

First, create a frame for the ghost by cutting out a circle of cardboard, as shown in Illustration 35. Make eye sockets from thin wire and attach them to either side of the circle. To attach the rod, bend it at one end and staple it to the bottom of the ring.

Drape the material over the frame. Glue enough material to the top half of the circle to keep the cloth in place. The rest of the material will then fall into folds. Cut holes in the fabric for the eyes. Then stitch them in place over the wire eye-pieces (see Illus. 36).

Moving eyes are not essential, but they can be very effective if you want to add to

the terror of your audience! The best way to make the eyes move is to have them attached to a separate wire stem which

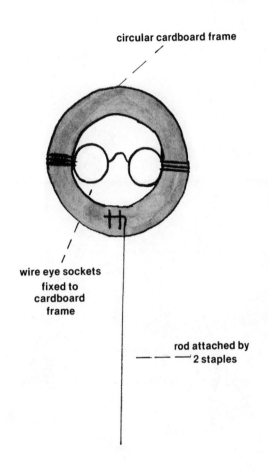

circular cardboard frame

wire eye sockets
fixed to
cardboard
frame

rod attached by
2 staples

Illus. 35. Wire and cardboard frame for ghost. The shaded part is the cardboard circle.

isn't connected to the rest of the puppet. Bend a piece of wire into a V-shape with two circles on the ends. Twist the base of the V into a Y-shape (see Illus. 37) to make a stem for holding. Bend the circles

33

at an angle so they will lie flat against the screen. Cover them with colored tissue paper.

When you operate the ghost, you can move the eyes independently of the body,

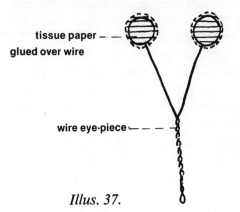

tissue paper —— glued over wire

wire eye-piece —— ——

Illus. 37.

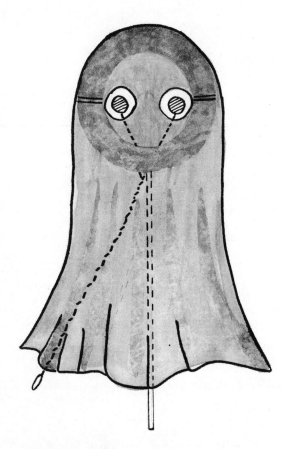

Illus. 36. Completed ghost.

or you can hold the wire stem of the eye-piece with the main rod. With a little practice, your ghost can give quite a performance!

Tropical Fish

Acetate sheet is an excellent material for the shadow puppet theatre. Its brilliant colors work splendidly with the light shining through them, especially as they are softened by the whiteness of the screen. Experiment with one color laid over another to get a variety of shades. This material is expensive, so keep even the smallest scraps; you can use them to decorate other puppets.

Cut the acetate sheet into fish shapes. Acetate is an awkward material to cut, so keep the shapes simple. Color some of them with glass-painting colors; decorate others with acetate scraps in a different color. Use clear glue to paste the layers together. Even clear glue will probably show, so try to apply it in a pattern which suits the puppet. Instead of attaching rods to these delicate figures, attach threads, and loop the threads over the

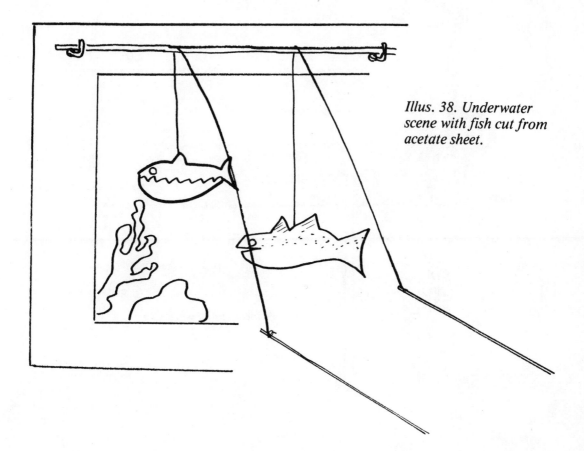

Illus. 38. Underwater scene with fish cut from acetate sheet.

horizontal rod at the top of the screen. The other end of the thread is fixed to a rod. This allows the fish some movement, which is splendid if they form the background of an underwater scene. They will be able to move vertically as well as horizontally. (If the fish have a leading part in the performance, you'll have to attach them to ordinary operating rods.)

You may want to arrange dried seaweed around the screen for a realistic effect. Scrunched-up paper and crumpled polyethylene (soft plastic) make interesting rocks. You can add real shells, if you have any that are the right size, or make them from cardboard.

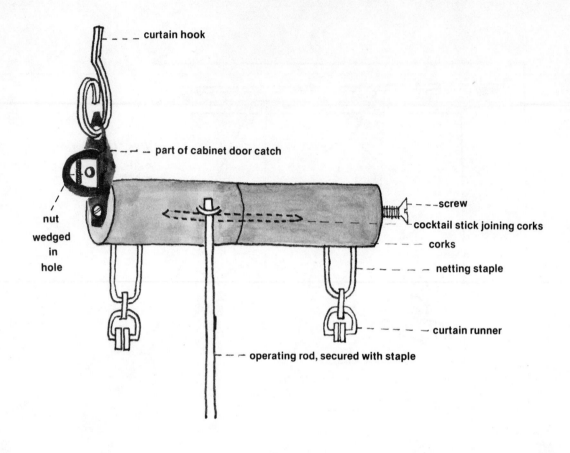

- - - **curtain hook**

- - - **part of cabinet door catch**

nut
wedged
in
hole

- - - **screw**

- - - **cocktail stick joining corks**

- - - **corks**

- - - **netting staple**

- - - **curtain runner**

- - - **operating rod, secured with staple**

Scrap Animal

Complicated as it looks, this strange creature is easy to put together. All the parts were selected because they were at hand when the puppet was being created. They are all pushed or screwed into the corks.

The appearance of this weird scrap animal is not very inspiring in daylight, but cast as a shadow on your screen, it becomes a lovable character with a distinctive jangling trot as its curtain-ring hoofs swing to and fro. This puppet is an example of a three-dimensional figure being used to produce a shadow—unlike the flat figures we normally use for shadow puppets.

These three—the ghost, the tropical fish and the scrap animal—are just a few experiments in shadow puppet design. You can come up with dozens of your own. The title of your play may suggest ideas. Household scissors have been used successfully in a shadow performance of a Scissors Ballet, for example. Once you start working with these puppet figures, you'll discover startling shadow shapes everywhere. Try putting them together, taking them apart. Use bits and pieces of scrap materials. Test them on your screen. The opportunities for creativity are unlimited.

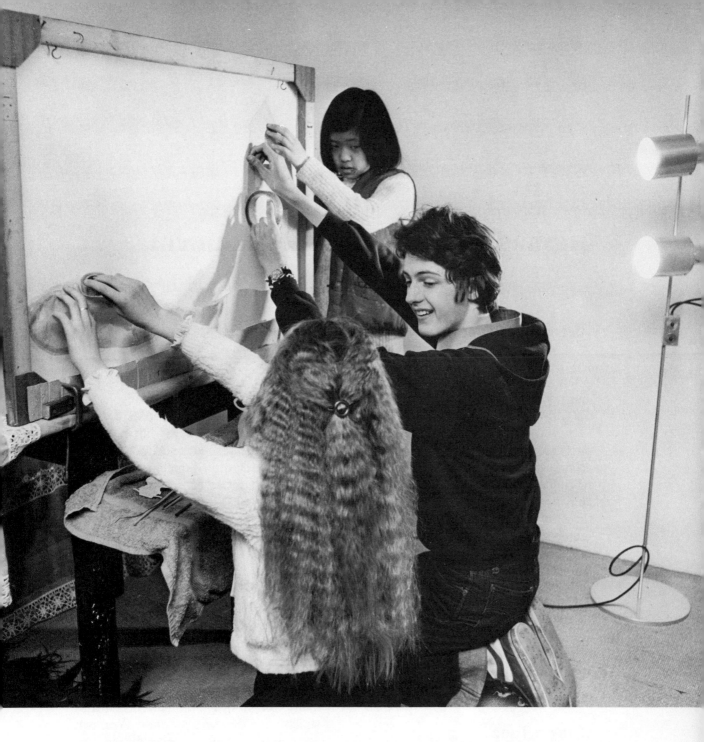

Illus. 40. Changing scenery — At the end of each scene, put on the house lights and turn off the operating light. Then, from the audience's point of view, the screen will look like a plain white sheet and you'll be able to change your set without being seen. The house lights will give you plenty of light.

4. Shadow Puppet Entertainment

Your puppet performance may be a play or a concert which you rehearse for several weeks. It may just as well be an entertainment you and your friends plan, make the puppets for, and produce all in the course of an afternoon.

If you already have some shadow puppets, you can probably weave a story around them, and after a couple of rehearsals, you'll be ready for your audience. For instance, the operators of the dragon puppet (seen in some photographs and on the cover) put on an impromptu performance, based on a Chinese story, immediately after they completed the puppet.

Here are a few ideas for puppet performances which can form the acts in a concert or revue. Generally, short pieces are more suited to the shadow theatre than the sustained action of a full-length play.

Using a Tape or Cassette Recorder

If you can record the sound track for your shadow entertainment beforehand, this will allow you to concentrate on working the puppets during the performance. It also makes it possible to use a greater range of sound effects and voices.

Friends and family who may not have time to take part in your puppet show may agree to take part in a play-reading which you can record. You might even want to include the well-known voices of television personalities, pop singers, or even politicians. (You can only use these for private performances at home, not for public presentation, which might involve you in paying fees.)

It also means you can have good sound effects and music just when you want them. It's reassuring to know that your tape recorder will produce a thunder clap immediately after the witch has cast her magic spell, so you don't have to prop up the witch against her cauldron and dash off to shake a sheet of cardboard to make the sound of thunder. In this way, a tape recorder helps to keep the action flowing smoothly.

You can also use records. There are many recordings of children's stories which your puppets can mime. You can play music from records during the performance or transfer it to tape. If you are playing to a large audience, you'll need to amplify the sound. This requires more sophisticated equipment than the ordinary small cassette recorder which is fine for performances at home or in the classroom.

38

Ballet

One funny way to use music in the shadow theatre is to produce a ballet. It's easy enough to find records of well-known ballet music, and you can make figures like the Ballet Dancer on page 23. Group puppets for the ballet corps will cut down some of the operating difficulties. A ballet also gives you a chance to show off your skill as a scene designer. Graceful woodlands, using real or pressed flowers and leaves, provide delightful settings for puppets.

The design on this page could be the background for many ballets. The grass is cut from green cardboard or paper, with a blue paper lake set in it. The fir trees are made of black cardboard or paper. Keep them tall and thin, so that they don't take up too much of the screen. They are there only to provide a decorative border. The flowers on the right are yellow primroses, pressed between layers of blotting paper.

Pressing Flowers

When you press flowers, it is important to get them as flat as possible. This is easier if you press the flower and stem separately. In the case of primroses, and many other flowers, you will still be left with a sepal behind the petals. Remove it altogether, so that the petals lie flat on the blotting paper. Cover them with another layer of blotting paper, and place the two layers with the flowers between them inside the pages of a book. Top it with a pile of books to provide enough weight to press the flowers. About three weeks later, arrange the flowers on the sticky side of a piece of clear self-adhesive vinyl (the sort sold for covering books). Use another piece of the vinyl as backing, or stick the first one straight onto the screen. One piece of the vinyl sheet and a layer of white tissue paper will work well, too. The natural colors of the flowers are beautiful on the screen.

Illus. 41. Woodland scene.

If you don't have time to press the flowers this way, you can speed the process by gently ironing the blotting paper layers. Then your flowers will be ready in a few hours. Note: this quick method doesn't work equally well with all flowers.

The bush on the left of the woodland scene is a piece of yew. Choose a flat piece and prop it against the screen. You can use other leaves, flowers and ferns, too.

The sun is orange tissue paper, attached to the screen by tiny white stitches or with transparent tape.

The cloud is white tissue paper or greaseproof paper, painted white and pink and attached to the screen in the same way as the sun.

Instead of building up the scene from separate items, you may prefer to paint the scenery onto a large sheet of tissue paper.

Opera

If you have any records of operas, you can include a short operatic sketch in your entertainment. It is hilarious to see tiny shadow puppets performing with the enormous voices of real opera singers! Keep the sketch short and it will make up for the fact that there is not much action. Add some attractive scenery.

This is a chance to try a puppet with a jointed chin. The illustrations here show how to make the face with a separate chin section.

The chin section is connected by thread at a point behind the puppet's teeth. Knot the thread and then, using a needle, push it first through the chin piece and then through the puppet's cheek. Knot it again on the other side. If you give the chin its own operating rod, you can open and

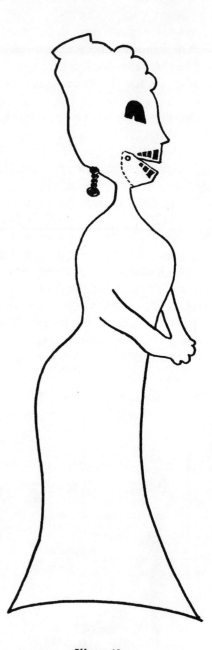

Illus. 42.

40

Illus. 43. Face with part of mouth cut away.

Illus. 44. Separate chin piece.

close the mouth to the music. Cut out the teeth clearly. You may need to trim the shape of the chin piece once it has been fastened, to make the movement as natural as possible. The prima donna's earrings are made from colored acetate sheet.

Political Speech

A separate chin piece can be used in a "head and shoulders" shadow figure of a well-known politician. You may hesitate at this idea because of the problem of making the puppet look like the person. This is not as difficult as it seems. Cartoons of well-known public figures

appear frequently in the newspapers and they will help you. Cartoonists are very good at finding and exaggerating those features of famous people that easily identify them. In your sketch for the shadow puppet drawing, aim for the same exaggerated outline, and you'll find that your audience recognizes the performer at once. You need, of course, to record the politicians' voices, but that is not too difficult, especially at election time.

Cartoons

Put on your own cartoons? You can do it easily, using a regular comic strip that runs in the newspaper. These cartoon characters are subject to copyright laws, so you can't use such puppets in public performances, but there's no reason why you can't use them for private shows.

This sort of puppet would be particularly useful with the small table-puppet theatre. You can set it up quickly to amuse a sick child, who would be delighted to see a popular comic character in action on the screen. It's a simple matter to adapt the story lines. They are usually straightforward, and by their very nature depend on visual impact and lots of action. Avoid plots with too many changes of scenery or complex settings.

Violin Solo

The puppet on page 25 is a violinist. He would be a good puppet to make if you have a record or tape of a solo violinist. Obviously, a serious musical contribution is impossible; it's best to play it for laughs! You can adapt this technique to other musicians. Why not make a set of puppets based on a popular rock group?

Illus. 45. Lynn is testing the chin movement while Angini holds the "head and shoulders" puppet steady.

Illus. 46. Here you can see how to redraw a simple cartoon figure as a silhouette. The character is still instantly recognizable and, if anything, the silhouette has greater impact. You can give it moving legs, if you want.

Poetry Reading

Poetry is an excellent source for shadow entertainment. The best poems for this purpose are those with a clear story and not too many characters. Before you start, make sure that all the actions required are possible for shadow puppets. For instance, if the puppet has to do some complicated action—like juggling or turning somersaults—the technical problems may be too difficult. It might be better to look further for a poem with a less ambitious story!

Edward Lear's poem "The Owl and the Pussy-Cat" adapts easily to a shadow puppet performance, and it's a good example of what you can do.

THE OWL AND THE PUSSY-CAT

I

The Owl and the Pussy-Cat went to sea
    In a beautiful pea-green boat:
They took some honey, and plenty of money
    Wrapped up in a five-pound note.
The Owl looked up to the stars above,
    And sang to a small guitar,
"O lovely Pussy, O Pussy, my love,
    What a beautiful Pussy you are,
        You are,
        You are!
What a beautiful Pussy you are!"

II

Pussy said to the Owl, "You elegant fowl,
    How charmingly sweet you sing!
O! let us be married; too long we have tarried:
    But what shall we do for a ring?"
They sailed away, for a year and a day,
    To the land where the bong-tree grows;
And there in a wood, a Piggy-wig stood,
    With a ring at the end of his nose,
        His nose,
        His nose,
With a ring at the end of his nose.

III

"Dear Pig, are you willing to sell for one shilling
    Your ring?" Said the Piggy, "I will."
So they took it away, and were married next day
    By the Turkey who lives on the hill.
They dined on mince and slices of quince,
    Which they ate with a runcible spoon;
And hand in hand, on the edge of the sand,
    They danced by the light of the moon,
        The moon,
        The moon,
They danced by the light of the moon.

—Edward Lear

Illus. 47.

Here are some suggestions for producing a puppet performance based on Lear's poem. You may not want to follow them exactly, but they may give you ideas, even if you choose a different poem.

Sound

If you can pre-record the sound track, it's an immense help, but it isn't necessary. Try to get one or two of your friends to work on the sound alone, without operating a puppet at the same time.

The narrators need to read the verse clearly and slowly with a good sense of its meaning. It helps if you can arrange a change of voice for the Narrator, the Owl and the Cat. The words, "O lovely Pussy O Pussy, my love" and so on in the first verse should be sung. If you can accompany them with guitar music, that will be even better.

In the second verse, after the lines:

"They sailed away, for a year and a day,
 To the land where the bong-tree grows"
you may want to pause and insert some

sound effects to suggest the sea. If you're using a tape recorder, experiment with water noises in the bathtub. If you live by the sea, you may be able to record the sound of waves breaking or seagulls screaming. You can get records of sound effects, too; your local public library may be able to help. Sometimes you can use the theme music for radio or television shows.

In the third verse, after the lines:

"So they took it away, and were married next day
By the Turkey who lives on the hill."

you could pause again to play wedding music, such as Mendelssohn's "Wedding March" from *A Midsummer Night's Dream.*

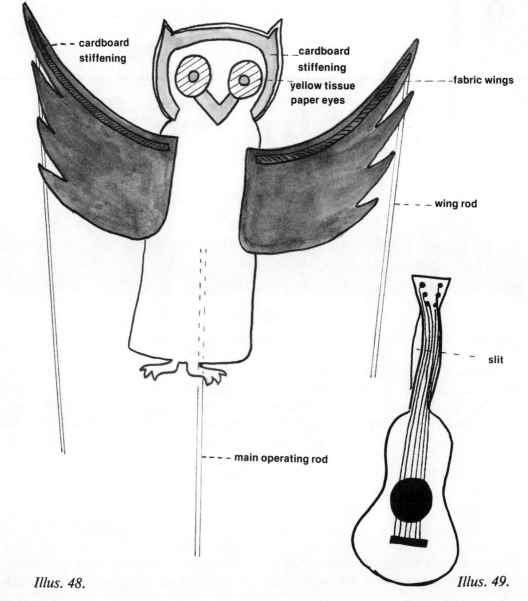

Illus. 48.

Illus. 49.

You can end the poem with any music that the Owl and the Cat can dance to – ballet music or disco or rock.

Puppets

You need four puppets: the Owl, the Cat, the Pig and the Turkey. The Pig and the Turkey have very little to do, so they can be simple silhouette puppets.

The Owl

The Owl has the most complicated action of all the characters – playing the guitar.

Cut the guitar from two pieces of white paper, decorated with felt pen. Glue them together, except for part of the neck of the instrument which you leave open so that the guitar can be inserted over the tip of the Owl's wing.

At the beginning of the poem, the Owl simply holds the guitar. When he starts playing, bend his wing tips behind his back and move him in time to the music. This will give the illusion that he's holding the guitar in front of him and playing it.

Making the Owl

When you choose cardboard for the Owl, try to get a soft brown effect. Using the small experimental screen, try out different stiff papers and cardboard to see how the light shines through them. A stiff brown envelope is effective, but it's a good idea to reinforce it with cardboard strips to keep it rigid.

Fabric wings may give your Owl the mobility he needs, but you'll probably have to glue strips of stiff paper along the top edges of his wings to prevent them from sagging. You'll need wing rods at the beginning of the poem, but you can remove them after the first verse.

To make the Owl's eyes prominent, cut out two circles. Glue yellow tissue paper over them. In the middle of each eye, glue a smaller cardboard circle.

The Cat

The Cat needs to be able to dance and hold a spoon. Since the Owl is a front-facing puppet, their conversations will look more natural if the Cat faces slightly to one side.

A jointed paw will make the cat a better dancer, and a small slit in the paw will enable the puppet to hold the "runcible" spoon. Insert the spoon in the slit so that

Illus. 50.

47

the Cat can "eat" with it. Insert the spoon the other way and the Cat can feed the Owl. Green and red tissue paper at the back of the Cat's face will give it more character. When you choose material for the Cat, experiment all you want, but black cardboard is fine.

Cut the Pig from cardboard, the Turkey from stiff brown paper. You can draw in feathers with felt pen or paint.

Illus. 51. Turkey cut from brown paper.

Illus. 52. Piggy-wig with a separate ring.

Illus. 53. Boat scene for "The Owl and the Pussy-Cat" (see photo on page 45).

Scenery

The poem requires two scenes: one in the boat and the other on land. The boat needs to be large enough for the Owl and the Cat to sit in, but they don't need to move about in it. Don't forget the honey and the money!

Cut the hull of the boat from stiff green paper – peagreen, if you can find it. The sea can be a blue scalloped ground piece. Use tissue paper for the sail, the pennant, the label of the honeypot, the money and the moon and stars.

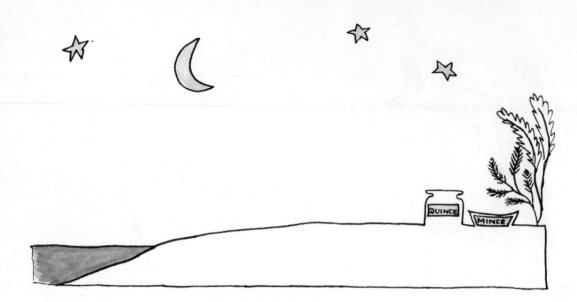

Illus. 54. Beach scene for "The Owl and the Pussy-Cat."

The second set, the beach, is used from the line:

"And there in a wood, a Piggy-wig
   stood"

until the end.

This set ought to have at least a suggestion of the wood in which the Pig lives. Flat evergreen branches, like yew, will do well. Place them on one side of the screen.

The beach can be a ground piece which slopes down to the blue tissue-paper sea. The beach must be the largest part of the scene so that the Owl and the Cat have enough room to dance on it, and to eat their mince and quince. Stars and moon remain from the first scene.

5. Christmas Entertainment

Since Christmas is the most popular time of year for shows and plays both in school and at home, it's a perfect time for a shadow puppet show.

Here are a few ideas for Christmas productions. Remember, though, that every puppet performance is a unique blend of ingredients. The type of audience, the number of puppeteers, the equipment available, the time for preparation – all these factors affect your choice of material and the style of production. Experiment for yourself and adapt ideas to fit your needs. The notes that follow are meant simply as jumping-off places – not rigid instructions!

A Nativity Story

There are at least two ways that you can present the story of the birth of Jesus. You can perform it as a straight drama, with the characters acting out the story, scene by scene. For such a presentation, you may decide to write your own play or adapt one of the many existing plays to the shadow theatre.

Another way to tell the story is to let the shadow puppets mime to the Gospel account. In this case, you'll depend more on the visual effect of the scenery than on the action. You can do a great deal of work preparing good scenery before-

Illus. 55.

hand, but the action during the performance itself will probably be within the scope of two or three puppeteers.

Here are some notes you can use for either version.

The text and the scenes

The birth of Jesus is told in the Gospels according to St. Matthew and St. Luke. You'll probably need to use both accounts. Here is a possible combination:

SCENE 1 – Joseph and Mary with donkey approaching the inn.

> Bible: St. Luke 2:1-7. Mary and Joseph travel to Bethlehem.

> Carol: "Once in Royal David's City"

SCENE 2 – Shepherds sitting on the hills, watching over sheep.

> Bible: St. Luke 2:8-15. The shepherds hear the good news from the Angel.

> Carol: "It Came Upon a Midnight Clear"

SCENE 3 – Shepherds in the stable.

> Bible: St. Luke 2 16-20. The shepherds visit the stable.

> Carol: "While Shepherds Watched Their Flocks by Night"

SCENE 4 – Herod's palace.

> Bible: St. Matthew 2:1-8. The Wise Men tell Herod of the birth of Jesus.

> Carol: "We Three Kings of Orient Are"

SCENE 5 – Wise Men enter the stable.

> Bible: St. Matthew 2:9-12.

> Carol and final tableau: with kneeling kings and kneeling shepherds: "Hark the Herald Angels Sing"

The carols provide convenient breaks for changing scenery. During this time, turn off the operating light and turn up the house lights, so the audience can join in the carols. During the last carol, you may prefer to leave the operating light on and bring the shepherds back for the final tableau.

52

Making the puppets

Mary

Traditionally, Mary rides a donkey to Bethlehem, so Mary and the donkey can be a single puppet for this scene. For the stable scenes, you'll need another Mary puppet in a sitting position.

Joseph

Joseph's actions are walking, leading the donkey and knocking at the inn door. His long robes will hide his legs, but a jointed arm would be useful.

Illus. 57. Mary sitting.

Illus. 56. Mary on donkey.

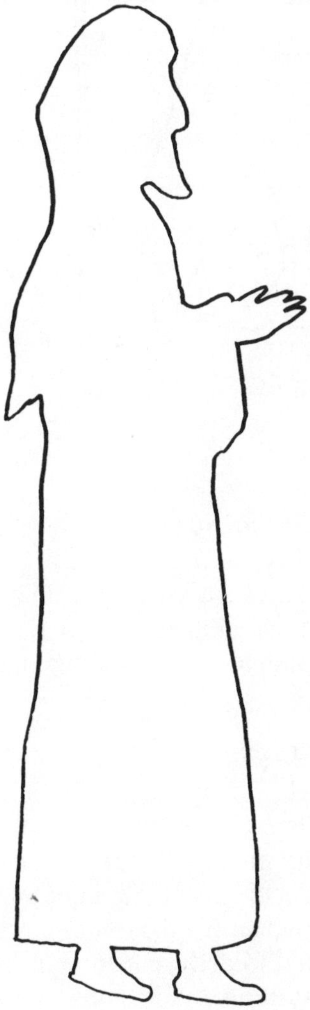

Illus. 58. Joseph.

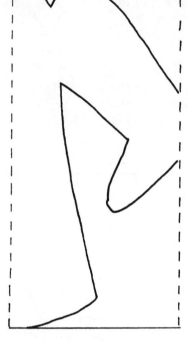

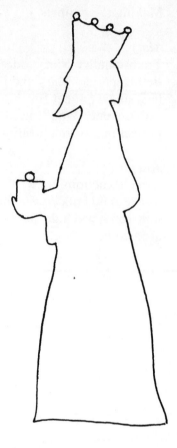

Illus. 59. Shepherd.　　　　*Illus. 60. Angel cut-out.*　　　　*Illus. 61. Wise Man.*

Shepherds

They have to be able to sit, walk and also kneel. Jointed legs (hip and knee), or, if their clothes are long, a jointed robe, should provide enough movement.

Angels

How many angels you have is up to you. The Gospel account indicates one main angel and a heavenly host. You may decide to make a single angel and a group puppet for the rest. You can do this with a folded paper cut-out – paper-doll fashion.

Wise Men

Like the shepherds, the wise men need to walk and bow or kneel. They can be formal figures with long robes. Probably the only jointing necessary will be at the waist or knee, and perhaps at the elbow or shoulder for carrying their gifts.

Innkeeper

This character is not absolutely necessary and could just as easily remain inside the inn. The incident could be represented by Joseph knocking, pausing and then turning away.

Illus. 63. Ass.

Illus. 62. Ox.

Ox and Ass
Plain silhouettes are enough. They actually form part of the scenery.

Herod
He could remain sitting on his throne with a simple arm movement.

Although a few outline shapes are illustrated here, you'll probably want to design your own figures. Christmas cards may give you more ideas. You need to decide whether to color the puppets or leave them black silhouettes; a combination of both is very effective. For example, try putting Mary, Joseph and the Angel in color and the other figures in black.

Illus. 64. Herod.

Illus. 65. Scene 1—Setting for Scene 1 of Nativity Reading.

Scenery

SCENE 1 – Mary and Joseph approaching the inn.

The sky is made from dark blue tissue paper. Cut out the star and replace it with yellow tissue paper, taped down with transparent tape. The buildings are white

cardboard, with black felt pen outlines. The inn has been colored with black felt pen.

SCENE 2 – Shepherds sitting on the hill.

You need a simple hill ground piece, similar to the one on page 14. You could replace the tree with sheep.

Illus. 66. Scenes 3 and 5 – The stable. Notice that there are very few props in these scenes, as they get quite crowded with characters.

SCENES 3 and 5 – the stable.

Here again the sky is dark blue tissue paper, with a cut-out star. The stable is a simple outline, leaving space both inside and outside the walls for shepherds, wise men, and the ox and the ass. It's best to cut the crib separately and place it to suit your setting of the scene. Real straw or wood shavings taped to the back of the crib and along the floor give a realistic effect.

SCENE 4 – Herod's palace.

The palace could be indicated mainly by Herod's throne, but some other device – a banner, for instance – would help to set the scene. The illustration of the Emperor's Palace on page 113 would do equally well for Herod's palace. Leave out the chandelier.

The action

This generally follows from the reading. The main consideration is timing the action with the words. But there's no reason why there shouldn't be pauses in the reading to leave the puppets time to act.

Christmas Legends

A wealth of material is available in this area, and books about Christmas customs will give you many ideas. How about something like this?

The Glowworm

Legend has it that originally the glowworm was a plain brown beetle. On the first Christmas she was in the fields near the shepherds, and like them she saw the angels. When she heard their message, she decided she must follow the shepherds to the stable.

She took with her her most precious possession – a hay seed she had been storing. Her journey through the long grass was hard work, but eventually she arrived and made her way to the pile of hay where the baby was lying. No one noticed her except Jesus who touched her gently with his finger. Ever since she has glowed with his light.

Glowworm Production Notes:

In the first scene you need a fairly small glowworm in order to include the shepherds and the angels. But for the rest of the story, use a larger glowworm. In the

Illus. 67. This drawing shows only part of the setting. It should be much wider than shown here, and it should include other obstacles, like stones and twigs, for the glowworm to overcome.

stable scene, especially, it isn't possible to keep the relative sizes of the baby and the glowworm in proportion. It is easier to have the Child resting on some straw and a fairly large glowworm pushing her gift towards him.

This tale presents a good opportunity to use a mixture of black silhouette and color. In Illustration 67, for instance, the shaded part of the long grass is green tissue paper and the stalks are black. The grass at the bottom could also be green tissue paper. The hay seed is black and the glowworm is brown cardboard. Choose a thin cardboard that will let the light glow through warmly. The simplest way to make the glowworm "glow" at the end of the stable scene is to make a second "glowing" figure. The glowworm can bury herself in the straw and then emerge transformed (though still recognizable).

Mistletoe

We associate many things with Christmas, though the connection is not always very clear: holly, Christmas trees, and mistletoe, for example. Any stories connected with them would be fine material for a Christmas shadow entertainment.

For instance, the Norse legend about Baldur the Beautiful, who was killed by a branch of mistletoe, lends itself splendidly to shadow dramatization. The story goes that Baldur, the son of Odin and Frigga, who were Norse gods, was the most loved of all the gods. He was as beautiful to look at as the dazzling sun.

One night young Baldur had a dream that he would die shortly. The thought of this depressed him so much that he went to his mother and told her about the dream. Frigga knew that Death had indeed cast a shadow over her son, and she decided she must do everything in her power to prevent Death's taking him. She was a powerful goddess. She went about the earth and made everything on it promise not to harm him.

When the gods heard this, they were intrigued, and they invented a new game which Baldur enjoyed as much as they did. Baldur would stand before them as they threw spears and stones at him. The weapons always missed Baldur. It was a good game.

NOTE:
Cut the weapons separately and let them fly through the air (attached to their own rods).

One god, Loki, was evil, and he discovered that there was one thing that Frigga had not bothered to protect Baldur from – the mistletoe. So Loki took a mistletoe bough and sharpened the end like an arrow. He persuaded Baldur's blind brother Hodur to join in the game. Hodur took the mistletoe and, with Loki to guide his arm, threw it at Baldur. It pierced the young god's heart and Baldur died immediately.

Frigga planted the mistletoe in a very high tree so that it could not harm anyone again. Custom has it, perhaps because of Baldur's sad story, that if mistletoe is used as a decoration at Christmas, it must be hung from the ceiling, so that it cannot touch the ground or the walls of our houses.

There are many other superstitions about mistletoe. Some people believe it has the ability to heal. The custom of kissing under the mistletoe is very old and probably dates back to its connection with ancient fertility rites. You rarely see mistletoe used as a decoration in churches; church authorities at one time forbade anyone to bring it into a church building – because of its ancient pagan association. It looks as if you could practically produce a complete Christmas entertainment based on mistletoe!

Santa Claus

His striking red clothes make Santa Claus an excellent subject for the shadow screen, and there are many ways you can introduce him. You can go back to the legends about St. Nicholas, and tell how he provided dowries for the sisters who might otherwise have been sold as slaves, since their father was too poor to provide a marriage dowry.

You may prefer a modern Santa Claus, complete with reindeer flying through the sky. This effect is easier to produce with shadow puppets than in other puppet theatres! You could write your own Santa Claus story or use an existing one, such as Clement C. Moore's "A Visit from St. Nicholas" (sometimes called "'Twas the Night before Christmas") or the song "Rudolph, the Red-Nosed Reindeer."

Hanukkah

The Jewish Feast of *Hanukkah,* or The Festival of Lights, is celebrated for eight days, usually in early December. It dates back more than 2,100 years to the days when the tyrant Antiochus Epiphanes invaded Jerusalem with elephants, chariots, cavalry and a great fleet. He stripped the temple of its secret treasures and burned pagan sacrifices at the altar. He plundered and burned the city, taking women and children captive and massacring men. He burned the Book of Law and demanded that the people give up their religious practices and worship as they were told.

The priest Mattathias and his five sons fled to the mountains and became outlaws, organizing a guerilla band in the wilderness which became known as the Maccabees. Antiochus pitted huge armies against them, but they placed their faith in God and after years of fighting, drove out the invaders.

The Maccabees set about rebuilding the temple and when everything was ready for its re-dedication, they discovered that there was no consecrated oil with which to light the lamp which should burn day and night. A frantic search turned up only one single jar of holy oil, barely enough to keep the light burning for a single day – and it would take eight days for the priests to prepare new holy oil.

They poured the oil into the lamp. When they returned the next day, expecting the light to be out, they were amazed to see that it was still burning. And it went on burning, not just for one day, but for all eight days, until the new oil was ready.

Those eight days were declared a time of gladness and joy to be celebrated every year. And this is why, even today, many Jewish people light a candle on every one of the eight days of Hanukkah. They exchange gifts and children play with spinning tops marked with the letters NGHS. That stands for the words, *"Nes Godol Hoyoh Shom,"* which means "The great miracle happened here."

The battles between Antiochus and the Maccabees are difficult to stage on the shadow puppet screen, but the rest of the story can be dramatized very effectively.

There are many Jewish folktales which you can also use for an entertainment at this time of year. Here is an animal fable that appears in many versions – not only in Jewish folklore – but in many other cultures as well.

The Wise Bird and the Foolish Man

A man caught a bird in a big net.

The bird said, "Let me go and I will give you three very useful pieces of advice."

"When you have told them to me, I will let you go," said the man.

The bird replied, "First, never regret the past. Second, never believe the unbelievable. Third, never seek to obtain the unattainable. Now I have taught you wisdom. Let me go as you promised."

The man let the bird fly away.

She perched in a nearby tree and called to him, "Foolish man! You let me go without realizing I carry in my body a pearl, very valuable, and through whose magic power I have learned wisdom."

The man bitterly regretted that he had let the bird escape, and he began to climb the tree. But a branch broke, and he fell to the ground.

He groaned in pain.

The bird laughed and said, "You fool! Did I not give you three pieces of advice? First, I told you, never regret the past, and immediately, you regretted letting me go. Second, I said that you should never believe the unbelievable, yet you believed me when I told you a silly story about carrying a pearl in my body. Third, I told

you never to seek to obtain the unattainable, yet you started up this tree to try to catch me with your bare hands. Now look at you! How foolish can you be!"

This story is ideal for shadow puppets, and it can be performed easily by two operators. If you are able to use your screen with the long sides standing up and the short sides at the top and bottom, you'll make better use of space, but this arrangement isn't essential.

The bird has a moving beak and a moving wing. The man has one leg in two sections and a moving arm. You could attach rods to the man's moving foot, his moving hand and body, and to the bird's wing, beak and body.

The net (not illustrated) could be made with plastic netting and a cardboard frame – like the hen's string bag on page 76. Or you could twist a piece of wire into the shape of a tennis racquet frame and either stretch plastic net over it or criss-cross it with pieces of thread. This would provide the man with a sort of giant butterfly net.

Cut the breaking branch separately and secure it to the tree with a paper fastener. You can make it *break* (not come away completely) by pulling hard on a piece of thread tied to the branch.

Illus. 68. The wise bird and the foolish man.

6. The Little Red Hen

Choosing Material for Shadow Puppet Plays

Here are a few guidelines to help you choose material for shadow puppet plays. There are a few main questions to ask yourself.

1. How many puppeteers and helpers are available and what are they capable of doing? Are you going to pre-record the sound or will the operators have to speak?
When you have answered these questions, you'll have some idea of what sort of play to choose. Plays with large casts, all of whom are on stage at one time, won't work, since there is a limit to the number of puppeteers you can squeeze behind even the largest screen – and a limit to the number of puppets you can get on the screen.

Run through the plot to see if there will be more puppets on the screen at any one time than there are operators to work them. Don't forget that if you have a shelf for propping rods, you can have one operator working several puppets, as long as they don't move at the same time. If one character is always on stage, will its operator's knees and arms get tired? Can someone else take over?

2. What are the technical problems? Can your group handle them?
For instance, a fireworks display on the screen is probably beyond the ingenuity of most people, though if you have a budding electrical engineer among you, he or she may want to experiment with lights masked by revolving discs. It has been done!

But if the technical side isn't your company's strong point, it's probably best to avoid wars or fires or stories where characters change color frequently or have to perform delicate operations with their hands.

3. Is there the right amount of action?
A story that is all talk and no action is not visually exciting. On the other hand, too *much* action, especially if it requires great skill from the puppeteers, may be too difficult to perform well. Make sure the play you choose is within your scope.

4. Is the action in the right place?
It's best to avoid stories that have frequent and complicated scene changes or long journeys which require more movement than a shadow puppet screen allows.

5. Can you adapt the material into a dramatic form that suits shadow puppets?
First, a play needs a shape, a dramatic shape. It needs to build up to a climax and then end in a way which is satisfying to the audience. In other words, you should be

able to tie up all the ends and leave no unanswered questions.

When you adapt material into a shadow puppet play, make sure that the characters can convey all the information the audience needs in order to understand the plot. If long explanatory speeches are needed, it holds up the action.

The best way to work when you're writing your own shadow puppet play is to proceed gradually. Start with a simple story, a straightforward plot involving two or three characters and a single setting. Once you've mastered the problems it presents, you're ready to move on to something more ambitious – like poetry, folktales, fables, Bible stories, legends, tales from history, or nursery stories like the following.

THE LITTLE RED HEN

An adaptation in dramatic form of a well-known folktale.

CHARACTERS

HEN
CAT
RAT
PIG
MILLER
BAKER

NOTE

Although there are six characters in this play, it can be produced easily by three puppeteers. The Hen is the main character, and she needs her own operator . A second operator can manage the Cat, the Miller and the Baker. A third can manipulate the Rat and the Pig. If you are able to record the play, along with music and pauses for action and scene changes, you won't need any additional helpers. If you do the performance "live," you'll need to recruit some friends to read the parts and operate the record player.

SCENE 1 – THE FARMYARD

(Enter LITTLE RED HEN.*)*

HEN: My name is Matilda, and I am a little red hen. I live in the farmyard with the Cat –

(Enter CAT.*)*

CAT: That's me! Meow! Meow!

64

HEN: — the Rat —

(Enter RAT.)

RAT: That's me! Squeak! Squeak!

HEN: — and the Pig.

(Enter PIG.)

PIG: That's me! Oink! Oink!

HEN: I am a very hardworking and industrious hen, and they are all lazy, indolent good-for-nothings, as you shall see.

CAT:
RAT: } Rubbish! Rubbish!
PIG:

(Background music starts as CAT, RAT and PIG exit. HEN pecks around the farmyard with a busy, dusting movement. Music fades.)

HEN: I am a happy little hen. I dust and I clean all day long, and I sing to pass the time.

(HEN sings — see page 70 — as she dusts. At the end of her song, she finds wheat lying on the ground.)

HEN: What's this I've found on the ground? My goodness me, it's some grains of wheat! Cat, Rat, Pig! Come quickly!

(Enter CAT, RAT and PIG.)

Come and help me! These grains of wheat must be planted at once!

CAT: I cannot help, my dear.

(Exit CAT.)

RAT: Nor I, my dear.

(Exit RAT.)

PIG: Nor I, my dear.

(Exit PIG.*)*

HEN: Oh me, oh my! what shall I do?
      Will no one help, not one of you?
      These grains of wheat, I'll plant alone.
      It doesn't help to moan and groan.

*(*HEN *picks up wheat stalk and exits.)*

SCENE 2 – THE FIELD

*(*HEN *enters with wheat stalk which she drops on the ground. Background music – planting song – starts as she pecks at the grains and plants them. She stops to admire her work.)*

HEN: That's a good job well done. With sun and rain, my crop will grow strong.

(Music continues and the wheat grows – see page 76 – HEN *moves to middle of screen.)*

HEN: The wheat is now full grown, and harvest time is here. I'll ask my friends to help me reap. Won't they be proud to harvest such a beautiful crop!

(Enter CAT.*)*

CAT: Hello, Little Red Hen. Your wheat is fine and strong.

HEN: Will you help me cut it, Cat?

CAT: Not I, dear Hen, for I have other things to do.
      My aunt is coming soon for tea,
      And then we're off to a jamboree!
      Farewell, dear Hen.

(Exit CAT.*)*

HEN: *(sighing)* Oh, dear!

(Enter RAT.*)*

RAT: Hello, Little Red Hen. Your wheat is yellow and ripe.

HEN: Will you help me cut it, Rat?

RAT: Not I, dear Hen, for I have other things to do.
I need to make a daisy chain.
Life is such a terrible strain.
Farewell, dear chick.

(Exit RAT.*)*

HEN: *(sighing)* Oh, dear!

(Enter PIG.*)*

PIG: Hello, Little Red Hen. Your wheat is plump and mature.

HEN: Will you help me cut it, Pig?

PIG: Not I, dear Hen, for I have other things to do.
I have a date with a bumblebee
Who wants to make a friend of me.
Farewell, dear fowl.

(Exit PIG.*)*

HEN: *(sighing)* Oh, dear! I shall have to cut it myself.

(She picks up a knife and starts to cut the wheat.)

SCENE 3 – THE FARMYARD

*(*CAT, RAT *and* PIG *are already on stage. Enter* HEN.*)*

HEN: Dear friends, will you help me carry the wheat to the mill?
The Miller will grind it into flour.

CAT:
RAT: } We are far too busy!
PIG:

> *(CAT, RAT and PIG sing and dance. HEN watches them for a while. In the middle of their song, she goes off sadly.)*

CAT: Well, now, what shall we do next? We've danced and we've sung.

RAT: We've been so busy, I'm exhausted.

PIG: Oink! Oink! I'm puffing and blowing. I must have a rest!

CAT: That, friends, is our next job – a rest. Imagine that silly Hen asking us to help her when we're so busy!

RAT: Where could we get the time?

PIG: I'm worn out. I'm off to bed!

> *(Exit PIG.)*

RAT: So am I!

> *(Exit RAT.)*

CAT: So am I!

> *(Exit CAT. Sounds of snoring are heard.)*

SCENE 4 – THE MILL

> *(The MILLER is standing by the windmill with a sack. He moves forward.)*

MILLER: I am the Miller, the man of the hour.
I am the one who makes wheat into flour.
I'm always busy, I'm grinding the wheat.
And when I'm finished I go home to eat.

(Enter HEN.*)*

Here comes my friend, the little Hen.
What do you bet she'll ask again.
Whether her flour is ready and good.
She's the fussiest fowl in the neighborhood.

HEN: Miller, is my flour ready?

MILLER: Yes, dear red Hen, your flour is ready,

HEN: Thank you, sir.

> *(*HEN *picks up the sack in her beak. Exit* MILLER. *Enter* CAT, RAT *and* PIG.*)*

CAT:
RAT: } Dear Hen, what have you there?
PIG:

HEN: Flour. The Miller has ground my wheat into flour.

CAT:
RAT: } And what are you going to do with it now?
PIG:

HEN: Bake it into bread, of course. Will you, dear friends, help me take it to the Baker?

CAT: Tomorrow I may.

RAT: Next week, I say.

PIG: I'm afraid – not today.

> *(Enter* BAKER.*)*

BAKER: Right now, I say! Come, Little Red Hen, and I'll bake you a loaf to be proud of.

> *(Exit* BAKER *and* HEN. CAT, RAT *and* PIG *sing a song. At the end of the song,* HEN *enters, carrying a loaf in string bag.)*

CAT: What a wonderful smell!

RAT: What a glorious color!

PIG: What a splendid size!

(CAT, RAT *and* PIG *sidle up to the* HEN.)

CAT: ⎫
RAT: ⎬ Shall we help you eat it?
PIG: ⎭

HEN: Away with you! The loaf is mine! There's not a crumb for you!

(HEN *stalks out.*)

CAT: Oh dear!

RAT: Oh dear!

PIG: Oh dear!

(Background music)

THE END

Music

Think carefully about what you want the music to do. Do you want your audience to laugh? In this play, you certainly do. You can increase the comedy by the music you use. For instance, in the first scene you need a song for the hen to sing while she dusts. A song like "Whistle While You Work" (from the film *Snow White and the Seven Dwarfs)* would be good, but remember, if you're giving a public performance, you need to get permission from the owners of the copyright of the song you use. Just write to the publishing company whose name on the sheet music. This isn't necessary for performances you give at home or at school.

You might increase the comic effect even more by choosing a recording from an opera for the Hen to "sing" as she dusts, or some other song which is unlikely and unexpected.

In Scene 2, you will need a song or background music while the Hen plants. When she finishes her task, the music continues as the wheat grows. A work song would do well at this point.

In Scene 3, the song and dance by the Cat, Rat and Pig form an important part of the action. Choose something lively and carefree with a strong dance rhythm.

You need similar music in Scene 4. The music here suggests the passing of time while the bread is being baked.

In addition, you need background music for Scenes 1 and 4. Use something that is not too obtrusive. You don't want to distract the attention of the audience from the action.

Scenery

The play has three sets: the Farmyard, the Field and the Mill. Since you need to leave plenty of room for the puppets to move around in the middle of the screen, there is space for just one or two pieces of scenery at the side of the screen to suggest the setting.

You can use the barn with the wheelbarrow leaning against it to represent the Farmyard.

The black parts of the Farmyard are made of cardboard, the shaded part of brown paper. Draw the sacks and the pitchfork with felt pen. The windmill is used in Scene 4.

The Field needs no scenery at all.

The Puppets

The Hen

The Hen is the most important character. She has to perform some complicated actions, such as dusting, planting, and carrying. For this reason, she needs to be a jointed puppet. Make her in four parts joined together loosely with strong thread. She should be worked by two operating rods, which permit a great range of movement.

Illus. 69. The Farmyard.

Illus. 70. The Mill.

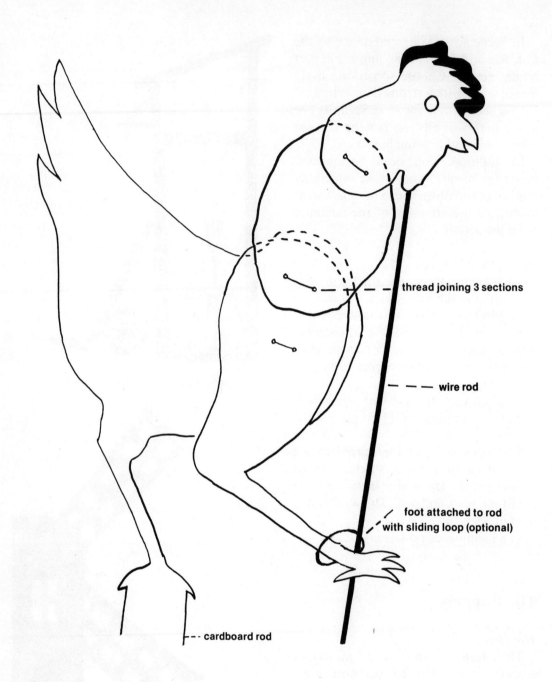

thread joining 3 sections

wire rod

foot attached to rod
with sliding loop (optional)

cardboard rod

Illus. 71. The Hen puppet.

Choose a sturdy cardboard for the Hen that will stand up to the wear and tear of rehearsals and performance. Use cardboard for one rod; it is a continuation of the main body section. Make the second rod from a wire coat hanger and tape or staple it to the back of the Hen's head.

With a little practice, you can develop very effective movements by manipulating the two rods. For instance, by crossing and uncrossing them in a scissors movement, you can make the Hen strut. By sliding the wire rod up and down, you'll get strong neck movements when the Hen is singing.

Finally, attach a hook to the back of Hen's head. This will enable you to slip the **wheat stalk**, the knife, the sack of flour and the string bag onto it without much fumbling. Make the hook from garden wire or cardboard and tape it securely in place.

Tape garden wire to the back of the Hen's legs to give them additional support.

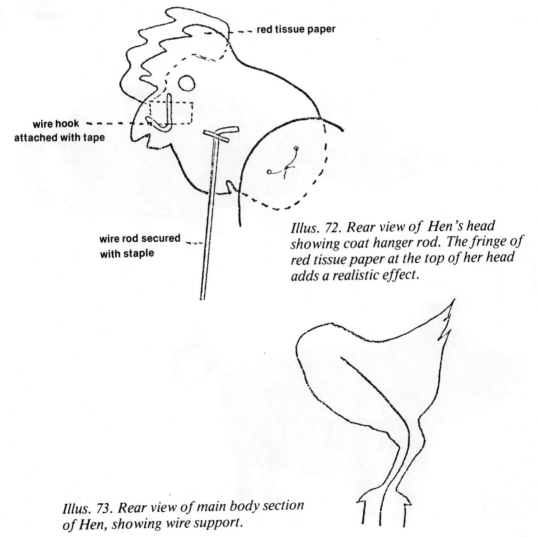

red tissue paper

wire hook
attached with tape

wire rod secured
with staple

Illus. 72. Rear view of Hen's head showing coat hanger rod. The fringe of red tissue paper at the top of her head adds a realistic effect.

Illus. 73. Rear view of main body section of Hen, showing wire support.

The Other Puppets

All the other characters – the Cat, the Rat, the Pig, the Miller and the Baker – have straightforward parts and can be simple silhouettes. Before you design and cut them out, decide which way you want them to face. It's probably simpler if all five characters face the opposite way to the Hen, though there is a case for having the Miller face the audience; he addresses them directly, and it helps to distinguish him from the Baker.

Illus. 74. Cat.

Illus. 75. Rat.

Illus. 76. Pig.

Illus. 77. Miller.

Illus. 78. Baker.

Props
Wheat

A real wheat stalk would do well. If you make it out of cardboard, bend the stem at an angle so that you can slip it easily into the hook at the back of the Hen's head.

The Growing Wheat

Make the wheat grow by gradually raising several stalks above the level of the ground.

A Knife

You can attach this by using the hook at the back of the Hen's head. A cross-piece between the hilt and the blade will help to keep it in place.

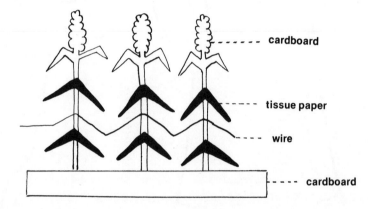

— cardboard

— tissue paper

— wire

— cardboard

Illus. 79. Cut the wheat as one piece from the cardboard. The shaded parts are green tissue paper. The wire, joining the stalks together halfway up, helps to make the piece secure.

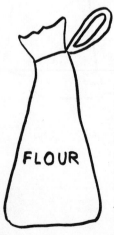

A Sack of Flour

Illus. 80. Draw the outline of a sack on thin brown paper and label it FLOUR. Add a loop of heavy thread with which you can attach it to the hook on the Hen's head.

FLOUR

Loaf in a String Bag

Illus. 81. The plastic netting that vegetables are sometimes packed in is useful in making the string bag. Stretch it over a cardboard outline of the bag. Inside the bag, the loaf should be visible.

76

Illus. 82. Shadow screen showing scene from "The Little Red Hen." The Hen is admiring her growing wheat .

7. The Lion and the Mouse

Fables are particularly good sources for shadow plays. They are generally short, have a strong story line, and provide a great variety of challenges for the shadow theatre. *Aesop's Fables*, especially, have much to recommend them. Here is a short play based on the well-known fable by Aesop.

THE LION AND THE MOUSE

An adaptation in dramatic form of a fable
by Aesop

CHARACTERS
LION
MOUSE
HUNTER

NOTE
Although there are three characters in this play, no more than two are on stage at the same time. This play can, therefore, be performed easily by one puppeteer.

SCENE 1 – THE FOREST
(Enter LION.)

LION: Countless days have I roamed; many miles have I travelled. I have skirted towns and scaled mountains. I have hunted; I have slain. I have crossed fast-flowing rivers and penetrated thick jungles. I have battled many foes. I have defeated them. *(pause)* Now must I rest. Here, beneath this broad oak will I lie.

(LION lies down. Soft background music starts. LION's eyes close. Enter MOUSE.)

78

MOUSE: *(flustered)* Hurry! Hurry! Mustn't tarry! My babies are hungry. There's danger about. Oh, what a to-do! I've lost my way.

(MOUSE looks around. She approaches the LION. Background music becomes menacing.)

MOUSE: How strange! I don't remember this hill being here.

(MOUSE starts to climb onto the LION and walks along his back towards his head. LION opens his eye. MOUSE peers down over his head and sees the eye.)

MOUSE: Oh no! It's not a hill at all! It's a — a lion's — a lion's snout!

(MOUSE falls off in terror. Background music ends on a discordant note. LION jumps up and raises his paw to the MOUSE.)

LION: Do you dare to disturb a lion's rest, you foolish animal? How dare you mock the King of Beasts with your impudent scrabbling?

MOUSE: Please, Sir King Lion, have mercy. You are so powerful and mighty that I mistook you for a mountain, begging your pardon.

(MOUSE bows.)

I crave your forgiveness. Do please excuse a poor feeble mouse.

(LION puts his paw down.)

LION: Very well, I will spare you. This time you are forgiven, but never let such a thing happen again.

MOUSE: No, Your Majesty! I will never, never do it again. And Sir, if there is anything that I can do to serve Your Majesty, I will be most pleased to oblige you.

(MOUSE bows.)

LION: A foolish thought. What could a mouse do to help a lion?

(Exit MOUSE. LION settles down again to sleep. His eye closes. Sleep music is heard in the background.)

SCENE 2 – THE FOREST

(Enter HUNTER, *carrying a net.)*

HUNTER: They tell me that the lion has been seen again in these parts. Long has it been my ambition to slay this proud beast. This is my plan. I will snare the lion with this net. Then, while he struggles, I will come with my gun and shoot him.

*(*HUNTER *arranges the net so that it hangs from the tree and reaches the ground. Exit* HUNTER. *Menacing background music starts.* LION *enters and walks into the net. He struggles and roars. Music reaches a crescendo. Enter* MOUSE. *Music decreases in volume so that the* MOUSE *can be heard.)*

MOUSE: Oh, mercy! What a fearful sound is that! It is my friend, the Lion. What angers him that he roars so loudly?

*(*MOUSE *moves closer to the* LION *and sees him struggling.)*

Oh, Sir King Lion, why do you roar?

LION: Little Mouse, what can I do? This net binds me fast. The Hunter is plotting to kill me. Soon I shall be dead.

MOUSE: Never fear, King Lion, I will set you free.

LION: You set me free! Come, do not mock me. How could a little creature like you help me?

MOUSE: Trust me, Sir, and you will see. My teeth are sharp and strong. I can free you from the Hunter's net. But first you must be patient and keep still.

LION: I have no other hope. I will trust you and do as you say. Come, Mouse, and do your best.

*(*MOUSE *climbs onto the* LION *and starts to nibble. She moves steadily along the* LION'S *back.)*

MOUSE: There's a split in the net from end to end. Now, Lion, you can escape!

*(*MOUSE *jumps off* LION. LION *gets up and the net falls about him.)*

LION: Little did I know – when I spared your life – that one day you would repay me and save mine. The power of a mouse is mighty indeed. How can I thank you?

MOUSE: *(modestly)* Oh, it was nothing. After all, one good turn deserves another. Good-bye, Sir Lion.

(Exit MOUSE.*)*

LION: I'll never forget that brave and tiny mouse. But look, who's here! It's the Hunter!

(Enter HUNTER. *He looks at the net, but does not see the* LION. *Menacing music starts.)*

LION: *(whispering)* This is my chance for revenge. I'll give him the fright of his life.

*(*LION *moves forward and roars.* HUNTER *lets out a piercing scream and runs off.)*

He won't go hunting lions again in a hurry!

(Exit LION.*)*

THE END

Music

In Scene 1, you need soft sleepy background music when the Lion is falling asleep. A lullaby would be fine. Replace it with more menacing music when the Mouse is in danger. You may need to do some experimenting to get the music to match the action; when you work out the score, tape it.

Use the same few bars in Scene 2, when first the Lion and later the Hunter is in danger. This will give shape to the production and emphasize the fact that all three characters find themselves in danger from one of the others. The "Ride of the Valkyries" from Wagner's opera *Die Walküre* and the Second Movement of Sibelius's *No. 2 Symphony in D Major* both have suitable passages.

The Puppets

The Lion

Cut the Lion's body from brown cardboard. Note the slightly enlarged outline of the Lion's head and shoulders (the broken line). Cut this out of yellow acetate sheet (or from two layers of yellow transparent adhesive sheet). It will give the Lion a sort of glow which will suggest his mane.

It isn't difficult to open and close the Lion's eye (see Illus. 84). You cut away the eye itself from the cardboard so that the yellow acetate shows through. The "eyelid" is a narrow strip of cardboard, just wider than the eye and at least twice as high. Bend the top half over to form a handle. Keep the eyelid in place with a pocket made of transparent tape. Line the middle of the pocket – the part which might stick to the yellow acetate – with a piece of narrower tape. The eyelid fits into this pocket. Make sure the pocket is tight enough to hold the lid securely, whether it is shut or open.

To make the Lion lie down, lower the puppet so that its legs disappear behind the ground piece and its nose nearly touches it. If you tack a cardboard flap behind the ground piece and near the tree, it will help you prop the Lion in position.

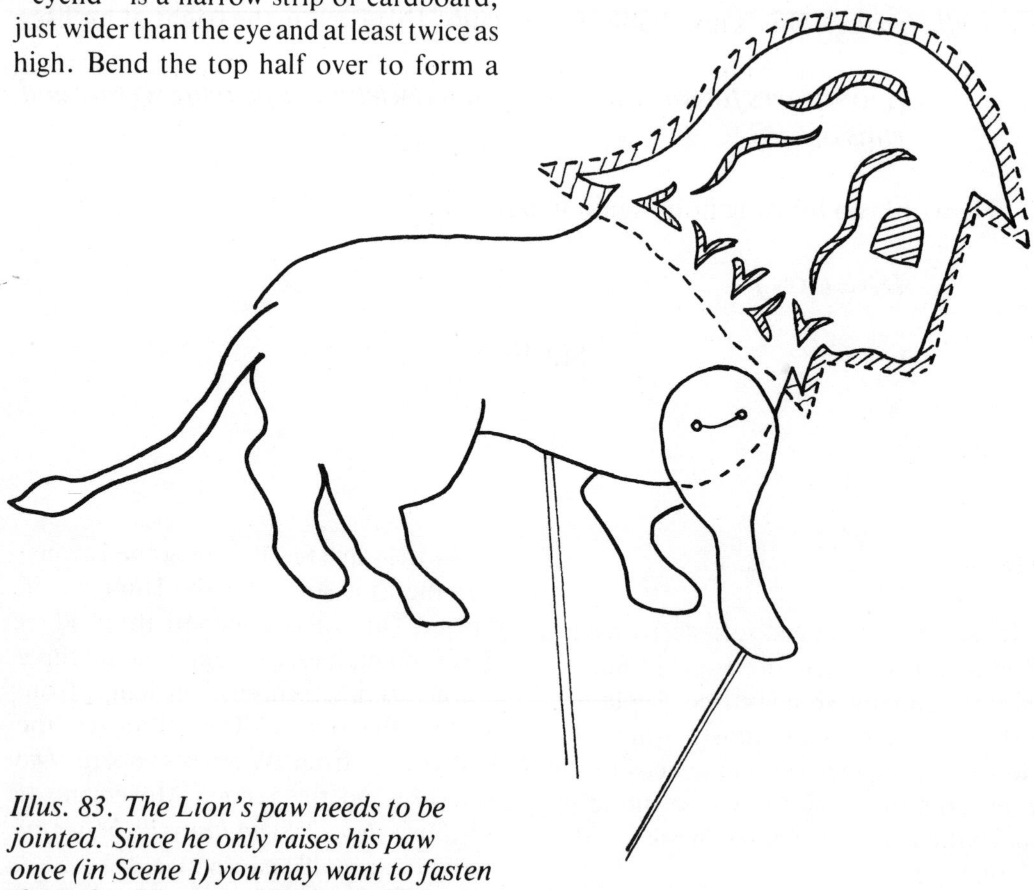

Illus. 83. The Lion's paw needs to be jointed. Since he only raises his paw once (in Scene 1) you may want to fasten the rod to his paw with a hook. This way you can detach the rod easily so that it won't get in your way for the rest of the performance.

82

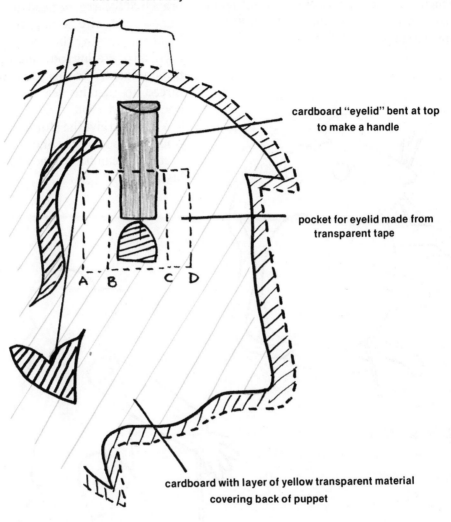

these sections shine through yellow where the cardboard
has been cut away

cardboard "eyelid" bent at top
to make a handle

pocket for eyelid made from
transparent tape

A B   C D

cardboard with layer of yellow transparent material
covering back of puppet

Illus. 84. Enlarged view of the Lion's head, viewed from the back. The pocket for the eyelid sticks firmly to the cardboard except between B and C, where it is lined with another piece of transparent tape. This enables the eyelid to move up and down without sticking.

The Mouse

The Mouse is a simple silhouette puppet which can be operated in an upright position for conversation or tilted at an angle to move on all fours.

The Hunter

Since the Hunter has to hang the net on the branch of the tree, he needs a jointed arm. Tape a small wire hook to the back of his hand for carrying the net. This arm also needs an operating rod. One leg also needs to be jointed. Tie this joint loosely with thread so that his leg moves freely; it doesn't need a rod.

You could give the Hunter a gun to carry when he appears for the second time in Scene 2. It can be fastened to the hook in his hand.

Illus. 85. Mouse.

Illus. 86. Hunter.

Scenery and Props

The forest is the only setting in this play. Since you won't be troubled by any scene changes, you may want to prepare some more elaborate scenery than in the previous play. You could use a paper screen and paint the scenery on it. Or you could paint it on a sheet of white tissue paper (the same size as the screen) and pin it to the screen.

In the illustration below, the ground piece and the tree are the only items not painted on the tissue paper. The tree needs to be sturdy enough for the net to hang from it. Cut the trunk and branches from cardboard. Glue green tissue paper to the branches for leaves. Two small pieces of wire, bent to form hooks, should be taped to the lowest branch. The net will hang from them until the Lion becomes entangled. The net needs to hang well and – eventually – drape itself over the lion. Cotton net will work more convincingly than plastic.

The rest of the undergrowth of the forest is painted on the sheet of tissue paper. Be sure to use very light brush strokes and leave a large area free in the middle, so that you don't hide the action. If you want to add pressed flowers, you'll find instructions on pressing and preparing them on page 39.

Illus. 87.

Illus. 88. Shadow screen showing a simple silhouette mouse puppet and a ground piece with tree.

8. The Emperor's New Clothes

Hans Christian Andersen's fairy tales provide a storehouse of good material for shadow puppet plays. Here is a musical version of "The Emperor's New Clothes," written for the shadow puppet theatre.

THE EMPEROR'S NEW CLOTHES

An adaptation in dramatic form of a fairy tale
by Hans Christian Andersen

CHARACTERS
EMPEROR
SPOT, *his dog*
PRESSANDMEND, *his valet (*PRESSY, *for short)*
QUEEN, *his wife*
RIP-EM OFF
PULLER FASTWON
TOWN CRIER
CROWD
CHILD

NOTE

The production of this play requires a great deal more of the puppeteers than the previous plays. The puppets need to perform some really complicated movements, and there are more characters to cope with. Even so, the play can be performed quite easily by four puppeteers. Three can manage it on their own if they use a shelf to prop the rods on, and pre-recorded sound. The play requires a screen at least as large as the one described in Chapter 2 (see page 9). It will also help if your back-stage working conditions are not cramped. Give some thought to where you are going to rest the puppets and props when they are offstage. The shelf gives you some space, but its main use is for propping rods. The space under the table, if you are using one, is a handy spot. If you have enough room for a chair or table behind the screen, it will help but it's not essential.

SCENE 1 – THE EMPEROR'S PALACE

(Enter EMPEROR *and* SPOT, *his dog.)*

EMPEROR: Come along, Spot, we must get going.

SPOT: What's the hurry, Master? I thought we were going for a walk.

EMPEROR: A walk? Oh, dear me, no, what an idea! Where's that valet of mine? Pressandmend! Pressandmend – where are you?

(Enter PRESSANDMEND, *known as* PRESSY.*)*

PRESSY: Here, Emperor, here I am.

EMPEROR: Pressy, I need four suits today.

PRESSY: Four, Emperor! Oh dear, what a job I have here!

EMPEROR: Of course, four! One to wear now, one for lunch, one for tea and one for supper. Bring them all in and I'll choose.

> *(Exit* PRESSY. *He returns, pulling a clothes rack. There are about 20 suits on it, all different shapes and colors. At this point there is a short conversation between the* EMPEROR, SPOT *and* PRESSY, *during which the* EMPEROR *holds various garments up against him. The conversation will depend on what clothes you've made. One or two ideas are given in the notes on page 116, but you will have more fun designing your own and then writing appropriate dialogue. Generally,* SPOT *thinks clothes are silly and at one point he says:*

SPOT: In my opinion, since you ask, the only possible thing to wear is a white fur coat with black spots.

> *(The conversation ends as the* QUEEN *enters. She is wearing patched old clothes.)*

88

EMPEROR: Here comes the Queen. I'll ask her what she thinks I should wear. *(To QUEEN)* My dear, will you advise me? What suits shall I wear today?

QUEEN: *(mopey)* How can you be so cruel? Just look at this dress! I haven't had a new one for years.

EMPEROR: Don't be unreasonable, Queenie. You know we can't afford new clothes for you when I have to have so many. It's silly to keep fussing. You look very nice as you are. Doesn't she look nice, Pressy?

PRESSY: Yes, yes, Emperor, though you did say I might get the tailor to alter one of your old robes for her.

QUEEN: *(angry)* Oh, did he, Pressy? Well, I don't want his old cast-offs. I've made up my mind. I'm writing for a mail order catalogue.

EMPEROR: A mail order catalogue!

QUEEN: A mail order catalogue, and all the bills will come to you.

EMPEROR: Oh, no, no, no! I won't pay them.

QUEEN: *(slyly)* I'll take the wheels off your skateboard –

EMPEROR: *(shocked)* You wouldn't, Queenie!

QUEEN: *(smug)* I would, and I'll ask my sisters to come and live with us.

EMPEROR: Don't bully me. I'm not paying –

QUEEN: And my aunts!

EMPEROR: Oh, all right then, on one condition. You let me get some clothes from your catalogue, too.

QUEEN: But of course, dearest.

(Exit QUEEN)

I'VE NOT A THING TO WEAR

to the tune of "Early One Morning"

EMPEROR

I've not a thing to wear, I don't know what to do! ____ I hate all my clo - thes, I find them ver - y bor - ing.

Chorus

Oh! who will help __ me? What a ca - tas-tro-phe!

How __ can you treat ____ a poor __ Emp'-ror so? ____

Verse 2

EMPEROR: **Satin and taffeta,**
And velvet, lace and denim,
I've tried all of them.
I find them very boring.

Chorus
Oh, who will help me?
What a catastrophe!
How can you treat a poor Emp'ror so?

NOTE

If you would like to get your audience singing, too, write the words to the chorus clearly on a sheet of white paper so that the light shines through it. Place the paper in the top half of the screen. You can do this with other songs in the play, too.

(At the end of the song, there is a loud knocking.)

EMPEROR: See who it is, Pressy.

(Exit PRESSY. *He returns with* RIP-EM OFF *and* PULLER FASTWON, *the swindlers.)*

PRESSY: Dear Emperor, an answer to your prayer. May I introduce two tailors, lately arrived in our kingdom from foreign parts – Mr. Rip-em Off and Mr. Puller Fastwon.

EMPEROR: Good morning, Mr. Off. Good morning, Mr. Fastwon. Did I hear my valet say you're tailors?

RIP-EM: Indeed, your Imperial Highness, that is our profession, and it is to you that we've brought our latest discovery.

PULLER: Yes, my Lord, your fame has spread far and wide. If I may be so bold, Your Highness, may I, a humble tailor, congratulate you, noble one, on your most excellent taste in clothes?

EMPEROR: Now isn't that nice? Did you hear that, Pressy? Don't you think that was a really charming speech?

PRESSY: Oh, most charming!

EMPEROR: Your words are the sweetest music that has fallen on my ears for many a month. Please go on. Indeed, I would like to hear more.

RIP-EM: Regretfully, noble Lord, if we were to sing your praises until the ending of the world we would not have time enough. Instead, may we explain the purpose of our visit? May we reveal, Imperial Greatness, why we have travelled hundreds of miles over mountains, across rivers, through –

EMPEROR: Yes, yes, forget all that. Tell me about this discovery of yours.

RIP-EM: *(solemnly)* Not only have we perfected a fabric of the most exquisite texture, design and durability, we have also imbued the cloth with a magical property.

EMPEROR: What? What? Tell me more!

PULLER: Clothes made from this fabric will give you great power. They will be invisible to anyone who is either unfit for his job or very silly.

EMPEROR: Great knickerbockers! What do you think of that, Pressy?

PRESSY: *(cautiously)* Well, Emperor, it sounds unusual and – er – it might have some snags.

EMPEROR: Snags! Oh, Pressy, you are such an old fuddy-duddy. Anything new and you mumble and grumble. I'm tired of your caution.

RIP-EM: Think, Your Greatness, what this will mean. Not only will you astound the world by the magnificence of this garment – and it is truly magnificent, isn't it, Puller –

PULLER: Oh, truly magnificent!

RIP-EM: You will also be able to tell without any difficulty which of your subjects are worthy to serve you and which ones are just fools.

EMPEROR: Marvelous, marvelous! These two young men are just what I need. They will revolutionize my wardrobe. Let them start work at once. Come, Pressy, you and I will inspect the attics and find them a suitable work room.

(Exit EMPEROR, PRESSY *and* SPOT.*)*

PULLER: Oh, ha, ha! It's worked, Rip-em! The vain old fool! Who would have thought our plan would work so easily?

RIP-EM: Now for an idle life! Food, ale and a warm room while we *pretend* to make the old idiot some new clothes. No one will ever dare say there aren't any clothes. They'll be afraid to look silly or lose their jobs. We've got it made, Puller!

FOR WE ARE OUT TO SWINDLE

to the tune of "For He's a Jolly Good Fellow"

PULLER and RIP-EM

For we are out — to swin - dle, We don't need thre - ad and spin - dle, We'll throw a - way — our thim - ble! And

Chorus

we shall not get caught, — And we shall not get caught, — And we shall not get caught, — For we are out — to swin - dle, We don't need thre - ad and spin - dle, We'll throw a - way — our thim - ble, And we shall not get caught. —

Verse 2

It's going to be so easy,
There's no need to be queasy.
Our clothes are somewhat breezy—
But we shall not get caught!

93

SCENE 2 – THE EMPEROR'S PALACE (A WEEK LATER)

EMPEROR: When did Mr. Off and Mr. Fastwon say my clothes would be finished, Pressy?

PRESSY: About the end of April, Emperor.

EMPEROR: Hmmm, the end of April, eh? That's wonderful. We'll have a May Day procession, and I'll wear my new clothes. I'll go from the palace to the market. We'll have tables of food in the market place so that everyone can celebrate. Let me see, we'll need trifles – and jelly – and mince tarts – and –

SPOT: And bones!

EMPEROR: Bones? We don't want bones. Don't be silly, Spot.

SPOT: Woof! Woof! We do want bones. I want bones. All dogs want bones! Bones are nice. Bones are good for you. Bones are best. Bones are –

EMPEROR: All right, all right, Spot. I've got the message – don't go on about it. We'll have bones. See how everyone takes advantage of me? Here's Spot demanding bones before I've barely said the word "celebration." Next thing you know the Queen will be wanting a new dress! Oh, dear me.

PRESSY: Cheer up, Emperor. You know it's going to be wonderful. You'll have your new magic suit to wear.

EMPEROR: Right you are, Pressy. I mustn't be selfish. We'll have a fantastic day.

OUR MAY DAY'S A SERIOUS MATTER

sung by EMPEROR, SPOT and PRESSY   to the tune of "My Bonnie Lies Over the Ocean"

EMPEROR

Our May Day's a ser - i - ous mat - ter, In -
spir - ing won - der and fear.___ Al - though I get old - er and
fat - ter, I'm smart - er than an - y - one here.

Chorus:
SPOT and PRESSY

Mar - vel, mar - vel, mar - vel your splen - dor to see, to see,
Mar - vel, mar - vel, O mar - vel your splen - dor to see!___

Verse 2

EMPEROR: **For years I have dreamed of this outfit —**
A robe set with jewels — with a hood!
The people will murmur about it —
"Oh, doesn't the Emp'ror look good!"

SPOT, PRESSY: *Chorus*

Verse 3

EMPEROR: **At last I will look like a winner.**
The word will go out near and far —
"The Emp'ror looks taller and thinner,
He'll soon be a big TV star!"

SPOT, PRESSY: *Chorus*

EMPEROR: *(Repeats Verse 1)*

SPOT, PRESSY: *Chorus*

EMPEROR: Now, Pressy, go to the attic where Mr. Off and Mr. Fastwon are working. See how they're getting on.

(Exit PRESSY.*)*

SPOT: I'm going too, Master. *(aside in a low voice)* I'm getting fed up with this "I'm the greatest" stuff. He's vain enough anyway without these tailors giving him ideas. *(to* EMPEROR*)* I'm off, Master. I'm going to see a dog about a man.

(Exit SPOT.*)*

EMPEROR: I hope Pressy finds some splendid work going on. Oh, dear, suppose he's a fool and can't see the new set of clothes! That'll be a pickle. I'll have to fire him, of course . . . Still, I'm fond of old Pressy, I'll find him another job. He could be – er – chief bootlicker! I haven't had a bootlicker for years. It'll be like old times.

(Enter SPOT *in haste.)*

SPOT: Master, Master, the Queen is coming! She's in a terrible temper!

EMPEROR: Oh dear, oh golly! Oh shabby, soup-stained socks, what shall I do!

SPOT: She fell over your skateboard in the hall and it's the 216th time!

*(*EMPEROR *hides behind* SPOT. QUEEN *enters on skateboard, balancing with difficulty and waving a wooden spoon.)*

QUEEN: Where is he?

SPOT: Who, your Majesty?

QUEEN: You know who, you whining, whimpering cur!

(The QUEEN *lifts the spoon to smack* SPOT. *He ducks and runs away.)*

QUEEN: I see him! I see him!

(QUEEN hits EMPEROR on the head. He falls down.)

YOU GOOD-FOR-NOTHING EMPEROR

sung by QUEEN and EMPEROR   to the tune of "The Miller of Dee"

You good-for-noth-ing Emp-er-or, How sil-ly can you be?___ Your on-ly care is what to wear, You nev-er think of me!___ I'll_ plain ig-nore a hor-rid Queen, I'll shout out loud, you'll see, ___ "I care for no-bod-y, no, not I, If no-bod-y cares for me."___

QUEEN: *Verse 2*
             You spend no time on deeds or state!
             You're full of vanity!
             You won't sign laws, you sleep through wars—
             You never think of me!

(She knocks him down again.)

97

EMPEROR: **I'll plain ignore a horrid Queen,**
(half-rising) **I'll shout out loud, you'll see,**
       "I care for nobody, no, not I,
       If nobody cares for me."

(QUEEN hits EMPEROR on head and he falls flat.)

SCENE 3 — THE SWINDLERS' ATTIC (THE SAME DAY)

(RIP-EM and PULLER are sitting on the floor, drinking wine. RIP-EM is holding a glass — fixed to his hand with soft modelling clay.)

RIP-EM: Well, this is the life, right, Puller? It was a good idea of yours to say we needed some wine to dye the Emperor's shirt.

PULLER: Yes, Rip-em, you might say we've got it all sewn up!

RIP-EM: All sewn up! Oh, you're a wit, Puller!

(The swindlers laugh uproariously. RIP-EM puts down the glass.)

PULLER: Now I shall do some work.

(He picks up scissors — see page 117. They both rise.)

Let me see, it's time I cut out the Emperor's vest. Hold up the fabric for me, Puller.

(RIP-EM holds out arms as though holding fabric. PULLER cuts the air. They laugh.)

RIP-EM: Splendid, Puller! You are a tailor of such style!

(There is a knock at the door.)

PULLER: Quick, Rip-em! Hide the glasses and the wine!

(RIP-EM kicks the glasses below the level of the screen. PULLER sits at the sewing machine.)

RIP-EM: Come in, come in.

(Enter PRESSY. RIP-EM *moves towards him.)*

PRESSY: Mr. Off and Mr. Fastwon, forgive me for disturbing you. The Emperor has asked me to call on you. He wishes to know how his new suit of clothes is progressing.

RIP-EM: Splendidly, Mr. Pressandmend, splendidly. See? *(snipping the air)* I am just cutting the Emperor's socks.

PRESSY: *(timidly)* Could I see something else, do you think?

RIP-EM: Of course, come over here.

(They walk towards PULLER *at the sewing machine.* PULLER *rises and holds out his arms as though displaying material.)*

PULLER: How about this? Isn't it fabulous?

PRESSY: *(pausing, while he peers closer)* What is it – exactly?

PULLER: Surely you can see it? It's the Emperor's cloak. Don't you think the background is an exquisite shade of green? Our theme for this cloak, as of course you can see, Mr. Pressandmend, is Spring. See here the snowdrops embroidered around the hem, and here – down the back – this pattern of daffodils and lilies. Here – mark the detail – a border of yellow chicks! It is indeed a cloak for May Day! Don't you agree?

PRESSY: Er – yes, it sounds marvelous. I mean – it *is* marvelous! Let me see, what did you say? I mean, of course, what am I seeing? A green cloak with snowdrops and yellow daffodils and lilies and chicks. Yes, yes, I'll tell the Emperor. He'll be delighted.

PULLER: You must excuse us now; we are very busy! Rip-em, we must unpack the pink brocade for the Emperor's waistcoat. Come.

(Exit RIP-EM *and* PULLER, *with scissors.)*

PRESSY: Oh dear me, what am I to do? I didn't see *anything*! Does it mean I'm a fool and unfit to be the Emperor's valet? There is only one thing to do. I'll have to tell the Emperor I saw the clothes and that they are magnificent. What a lucky thing Mr. Fastwon told me so much about the cloak. Green – with snowdrops, daffodils, lilies and chicks. . .

WHY CAN'T I SEE?

to the tune of "Poor Old Joe"

Why can't I see all the things that wise men see?

What will be-come of a sil-ly fool like me?

What would I do if the door a-gainst me shut? I

hear the Emp'-ror's voice ex-claim-ing, "Poor Old Nut." I'm

Chorus

stu-pid, I'm stu-pid, And there ain't no "if" and "but," I

hear the Emp'-ror's voice re-peat-ing, "Poor Old Nut."

Verse 2

PRESSY: How hard I'll cry! I will sniffle, snort and sob —
Oh, dearie me — when I have to leave my job!
Lonely I'll live in a crummy, slummy hut.
I hear the Emp'ror's voice exclaiming,
"Poor old nut."

Chorus

Verse 3
I'll have to lie and pretend that I can see
Cloaks, vests and suits, all as handsome as can be.
I'll praise the robes — yes — their fabric and their cut
So no one knows that Pressy's just a
Poor old nut.

Chorus

(Exit PRESSY. *Enter* SPOT.*)*

SPOT: Well, folks, I've just come to see what's going on here. No sign of Mr. Off or Mr. Fastwon, I'm glad to say. I'll just have a sniff around. Tell me if you see them coming.

(During the rest of SPOT*'s speech, if you want, the swindlers can return quietly. The audience will probably shout out.* SPOT *can turn and look, but when he does, the swindlers are gone. You can do this several times.)*

Not a sign of the new clothes. I thought when I saw those two that they looked like a couple of scoundrels. They're out to trick the Emperor, that's for sure.

*(*RIP-EM *and* PULLER *enter quietly.)*

No, there are no clothes here, I'm sure of that. But no one will believe me if I call them a couple of con men.

THESE SWINDLERS TWO

to the tune of "Little Bo Peep"

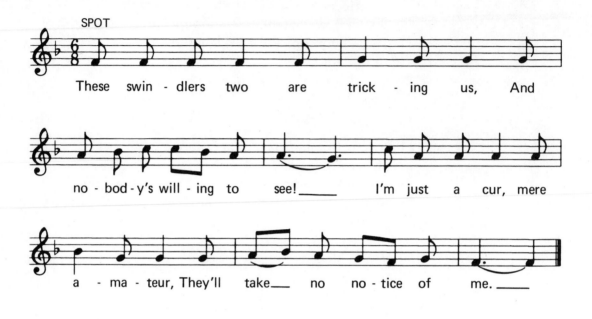

These swin - dlers two are trick - ing us, And
no - bod - y's will - ing to see! ___ I'm just a cur, mere
a - ma - teur, They'll take ___ no no - tice of me. ___

Verse 2

SPOT: **These swindlers two are tricking us.**
They've got my poor master agog.
Should I be strong?
Say they are wrong?
Why me? I'm only a dog.

RIP-EM:*(brandishing scissors)* No, they won't believe you, you impudent hound. Calling us con men, indeed!

PULLER: You know what happens to snippy little dogs, like you, don't you?

SPOT: *(squeakily)* No.

PULLER: We cut off their ears to line our shoes.

(RIP-EM lunges forward with the scissors. SPOT rushes out.)

RIP-EM: Do you think he'll tell, Puller?

PULLER: No, Rip-em. As he said, they won't believe him, and besides, we've frightened him now. I think we'll be safe.

(They repeat song "For We Are Out to Swindle" from page 93.)

SCENE 4 – THE EMPEROR'S PALACE (MAY DAY)

(Enter QUEEN, SPOT, PRESSY. *The* QUEEN *is dressed in an elaborate outfit with lace bows; see page 120.)*

QUEEN: Well, how do I look, Pressy?

PRESSY: You look delightful, ma'am. *(aside in a low voice)* Have you ever seen such a sight? She looks like an old fishing net.

QUEEN: It's a lovely, sunny day for the procession. A bit chilly, but we'll all be warmly dressed.

SPOT: *(quietly)* Except the Emperor.

QUEEN: What was that, Spot?

SPOT: Nothing, nothing. I just said I'm sure the Emperor will be a startling success.

PRESSY: Have you seen the Emperor's new suit, ma'am?

QUEEN: Oh yes. I thought it quite magnificent. Those crocuses!

PRESSY: You mean snowdrops.

QUEEN: Yes, of course – the snowdrops. And the blackbirds.

PRESSY: Could you mean the chicks?

QUEEN: Yes, quite so. It was all so splendid.

THE ROBES OF THE EMPEROR

to the tune of "John Brown's Body"

QUEEN, PRESSY, SPOT

The robes of the Emp-er-or, they are a splen-did sight, The robes of the Emp-er-or, they glis-ten in the light, The robes of the Emp-er-or out-shine each me-teor-ite, With en-vy we're all green. _

Chorus

Tru - ly, tru - ly, in - di-vid - ual! Tru - ly, tru - ly in - di-vid - ual! Tru - ly, tru - ly in - di-vid - ual! With en - vy we're all green. _

Verse 2 (hesitantly)

PRESSY: The robes of the Em-per-or — a glory of spring flowers,
The robes of the Em-per-or — a host of magic powers,
The robes of the Em-per-or will keep him warm for hours,

ALL: With en-vy we're all green!

Chorus

Verse 3

QUEEN: The robes of the Emperor are absolutely great.
The robes of the Emperor are certainly lightweight.
The robes of the Emperor make me proud to be his mate,

104

ALL: **With envy we're all green!**

Chorus

Verse 4

SPOT: **The robes of the Emperor are good for fun and play.**
                  They're marvelous for swimming and for boating and croquet,
                  They're sure to keep the breezes and the fleas and ticks away,

ALL: **With envy we're all green!**

Chorus

ALL: *(repeat first verse and chorus)*

(Enter EMPEROR during the last chorus.)

EMPEROR: How kind, how kind! The great day has arrived. I can't wait to see my new clothes! I'm glad I've kept them as a surprise. It's so much more exciting. Mind you, I was tempted. Oh yes, I was tempted to go and take a peek. Now, where are Mr. Off and Mr. Fastwon?

(Enter RIP-EM and PULLER, pulling clothes rack with row of empty hangers.)

QUEEN: How splendid it all looks!

PRESSY: It's beyond description!

(Exit PRESSY.)

PULLER: We have excelled ourselves, Emperor.

RIP-EM: Never has an Emperor appeared in such style before.

SPOT: I'll go along with that.

EMPEROR: *(peering at clothes rack)* Ooh! Aah. Aa-hmn.

(Enter PRESSY with a screen made of black cardboard which he moves to the middle of the screen so that it hides the rail of hangers. All the characters are on one side of the screen.)

PRESSY: Emperor, you can change behind the screen. Come along, sir.

(The EMPEROR goes behind the screen and appears on the other side. The other characters appear to be talking among themselves.)

EMPEROR: Oh, purple patched pullovers! What shall I do? I can't see the clothes! Am I a fool? Am I unfit for my job? Unfit to be Emperor? Jumping jodhpurs! What a catastrophe!

OH DEAR! WHAT CONSTERNATION!

EMPEROR
to the tune of "Oh Dear, What Can the Matter Be?"

Oh dear! What con - ster - na — tion! Oh dear! aw - ful vex - a — tion! Oh dear! What deg - ra - da — tion! What will be - come of poor me?___ I real - ize I'm use-less, I real - ize I'm sil - ly, The peo - ple should throw me out now— wil - ly, nil - ly. I've let them all down—Oh I'm real - ly a dil - ly, Oh, what will be - come of poor me?___

EMPEROR: *(repeats opening refrain)*

Well, it's no good moaning and groaning. It's perfectly clear what I have to do. I have to put on the clothes. Pressy and the Queen could obviously see them, so they must be there *(he moves towards the screen and then suddenly returns).*

How will I know if I've put them on? Grovelling garters! I might put them on back to front. I'd better get the Queen to help me. *(shouts)* Queenie, come here! *(he goes behind the screen).*

106

QUEEN: There's the Emperor calling. I'd better go and help him. *(Queen goes behind the screen.)*

(Exit QUEEN *behind the screen.)*

PRESSY: I wonder how the Emperor is getting on. He should be ready soon. Now I'd better explain about the procession. Spot – you shall lead it, followed by the Queen. Make sure she knows where to go, Spot. The Emperor will be next. Mr. Off and Mr. Fastwon, will you follow the Emperor? He specially asked that you should.

PULLER: Oh no, Mr. Pressandmend, we could not accept such a privilege. No, we'll stay here. Perhaps you could arrange for the Emperor to give us our payment before the procession.

PRESSY: Mr. Fastwon, Mr. Off, I must insist you join us. You can't disappoint the Emperor on this special day. And you might be needed to make some adjustment to the clothes.

RIP-EM:
PULLER: } We're sure that won't be necessary!

PRESSY: Ah, here is the Emperor.

(Enter EMPEROR, *the second puppet, without clothes.* QUEEN *follows.)*

EMPEROR: Well, how do I look?

ALL: Splendid, magnificent, marvelous, amazing!

SPOT: *(aside, quietly)* My worst fears have come to pass. I wish I had the courage to tell him, but I'm afraid of those swindlers and their scissors.

EMPEROR: I'm glad you all admire the suit. One thing, Pressy, before we go, can you arrange for the Town Crier to make an announcement in the marketplace?

SCENE 5 – THE MARKETPLACE

(The crowd is seen at the base of the screen; they are talking. Enter TOWN CRIER, *ringing bell.)*

TOWN CRIER: Friends, countrymen, pray silence! By order of the Emperor, all citizens are to take note. The Emperor bids me tell you this: Today our gracious Emperor will walk in procession to the marketplace.

107

(Crowd cheers.)

A new suit of clothes has been prepared for the occasion and the Emperor insists – I repeat – *insists* that every man, woman and child should know that this suit has special magic powers. It is invisible to anyone who is either a fool or unfit for his job. The Emperor further reminds you that you are all employed by him. So says the Emperor!

> *(Exit* TOWN CRIER. *Sound of processional music. Voices in the crowd shout out, "He's coming," etc. Enter small child from below screen. He stands just in front of the crowd – above them – and to one side. Enter the procession as follows:* SPOT, QUEEN *holding wooden spoon, naked* EMPEROR, RIP-EM, PULLER, PRESSY. *Crowd cheers.)*

1ST VOICE: Hurray for the Emperor!

2ND VOICE: How splendid is the Emperor's new suit!

3RD VOICE: The Emperor has surpassed himself!

4TH VOICE: Never has the Emperor appeared so gloriously clad!

CHILD: *(moving forward)* But he hasn't got any clothes on!

CROWD: Ssh – ssh, don't say that!

CHILD: But it's true. He hasn't got a stitch on!

CROWD: Did you hear what he said? Oh, how ridiculous!

CHILD: Can't you see? It's true!

CROWD: Hush, boy! You will offend the Emperor!

CHILD: Please – look at him!

CROWD: Well – maybe – perhaps you're right. You have a point . . .

CHILD: He's as pink as a newborn baby. *(laughs)*

CROWD: So he is! *(Crowd starts to laugh as well. Cry gradually goes up: "He's not wearing any clothes.")*

WHAT SHALL WE DO WITH A NAKED EMPEROR?

to the tune of "What Shall We Do with the Drunken Sailor?"

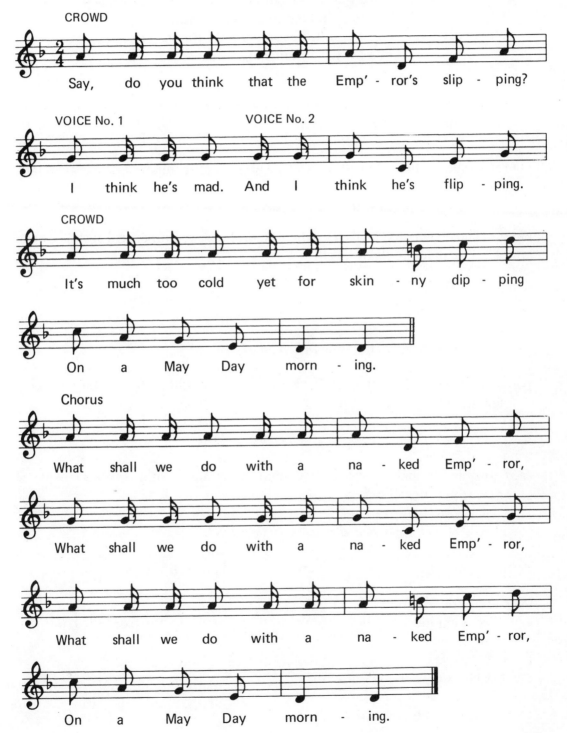

CROWD
Say, do you think that the Emp'-ror's slip-ping?

VOICE No. 1 · VOICE No. 2
I think he's mad. And I think he's flip-ping.

CROWD
It's much too cold yet for skin-ny dip-ping
On a May Day morn-ing.

Chorus
What shall we do with a na-ked Emp'-ror,
What shall we do with a na-ked Emp'-ror,
What shall we do with a na-ked Emp'-ror,
On a May Day morn-ing.

CROWD: *Verse 2*

Voice 1: Heard that those clothes cost him lots of money —
Voice 2: Well, he's in luck that today is sunny —
Crowd: Got to admit, he looks pretty funny —
On a May Day morning.

Chorus

(Repeat first verse and chorus. At the end of the song, the crowd raises its arms and cheers.)

RIP-EM: Come, Puller. Something tells me we should scamper before it's too late.

(Exit RIP-EM *and* PULLER *— fast.)*

PRESSY: Those swindlers! I'll chase them. Don't worry, Emperor. I'll catch them. They've made fools of us all!

(Exit PRESSY.*)*

EMPEROR: Fools, indeed.

(Enter TOWN CRIER *with screen.)*

TOWN CRIER: Here, Emperor, we've brought your clothes. Put them on quickly and then the procession and the celebration can continue.

*(*EMPEROR *goes behind screen.)*

SPOT: Just as I thought. I should have said something to him. I was a coward. I hate to see him so sad.

(Enter EMPEROR, *dressed — first puppet.)*

CROWD: Three cheers for our Emperor! Hurrah! Hurrah! Hurrah!

EMPEROR: You are too kind. I don't deserve to be Emperor. I've been vain and silly. I am unfit to rule. Those swindlers weren't so far from the truth. I'll resign.

CROWD: No, we want our Emperor!

EMPEROR: Well, do you really mean it?

CROWD: Yes, yes, we mean it!

EMPEROR: Well – in that case – I'll stay, since you insist.

>*(Crowd cheers and raises its arms.* PRESSY *enters with two ropes, tied around the necks of* RIP-EM *and* PULLER. *He is dragging them along behind him.)*

PRESSY: I've caught the scoundrels!

EMPEROR: Well done, Pressy! Now for their punishment. Shall I execute them?

CROWD: Yes, yes!

EMPEROR: No, I don't think I will. After all, they have taught us all a lesson. Let me see, Mr. Fastwon and Mr. Off, can you sew?

PULLER: We are – we were tailors, Your Majesty.

EMPEROR: Well, for a year you shall make all my clothes – *real* clothes, mind you. And you shall make the Queen three dozen new outfits.

QUEEN: Empy, are you feeling well?

EMPEROR: Yes, my dear, I'm quite all right. You know, I saw an absolutely super skateboard in your mail order catalogue and I wondered if you would get it for my birthday. Mr. Off and Mr. Fastwon, do you hear? This is your punishment. You are to work for me and for the Queen for a year and you will receive no payment. Remember, I could have had you executed.

RIP-EM: } You are truly merciful, noble Emperor. We are grateful for your
PULLER: } kindness, and it will be a privilege to work for you.

EMPEROR: And now for the hero of the day. Where is the little child who brought us all to our senses?

CHILD: Here, Sir.

EMPEROR: You, young man, shall walk with me in the procession. You shall have first helping at the banquet, and from now on you shall be known as "The Emperor's Most Sensible Advisor." Your birthday will be a national holiday, celebrated as "Wise Young Man's Day."

WELL THAT'S THE END

to the tune of "Auld Lang Syne"

Well that's the end, a hap - py end, The
mor - al is - n't new, That lies will fail if
one brave soul, Stands out and says what's true. So
fare - thee - well our friends, our friends, So fare - thee - well, a -
dieu. We hope you've liked our show to - day, Our
thanks to all of you.

THE END

Music

All the songs in the play are set to fairly well-known tunes, but in case you're not sure of them, check the melody line. You can sing them unaccompanied or with music.

Background music is not needed until the last scene. Here you need "procession music." The opening bars of all the following are good: Bizet's "Farandole" from the *L'Arlésienne* Suite, Prokofiev's "Troika" from the *Lieutenant Kije* Suite, or Rossini's "Overture" to *The Thieving Magpie*. Play the music for just a short while, until the song starts. When the characters are speaking, turn down the volume.

Scenery

Scenes 1, 2 and 4 take place in a room in the palace. Try to give the screen a "palace-like" look, but leave plenty of room for the action. You could use a pillar, a chandelier and a banner to get the royal effect.

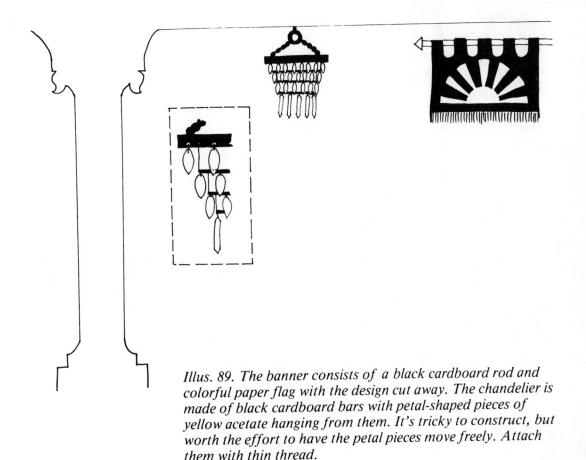

Illus. 89. The banner consists of a black cardboard rod and colorful paper flag with the design cut away. The chandelier is made of black cardboard bars with petal-shaped pieces of yellow acetate hanging from them. It's tricky to construct, but worth the effort to have the petal pieces move freely. Attach them with thin thread.

Illus. 90. Scenery for the swindler's attic.

Scene 3 takes place in the swindlers' attic. The beams at the top give the impression of an attic. You need plenty of room for the action.

Draw the sewing machine onto a sheet of white paper and cut it out. The clothes rack is similar to the one used in the earlier scene (see page 116); only half of it shows in order to save space. Cut the stool out of cardboard. Use tape to keep the outlines firm against the screen, except at the base, where you can slip the pieces in between the screen and the frame.

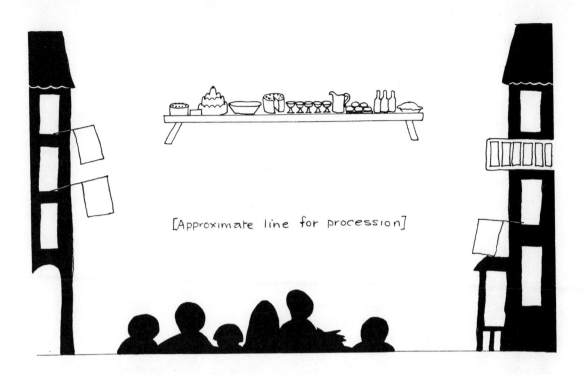

[Approximate line for procession]

Illus. 91. Scenery for the marketplace.

Scene 5 is the marketplace, and here the action takes place in the middle of the screen. At the top, as though on the far side of the marketplace, is a table, prepared for the feast. You can draw and color it on a strip of white paper and then attach it to the screen with transparent tape. The houses on either side can be black silhouettes or cut from white cardboard and colored in.

The bottom of the screen is taken up by the crowd. Make the crowd in the form of a group puppet with moving arms. It's probably most effective as a black silhouette.

In this scene all the characters, except the Child, act on an imaginary line in the middle of the screen. This imaginary line is indicated by the words "Approximate line for procession."

Props

For the scenes in the palace, you'll need:

> a clothes rack with hangers
> clothes
> a wooden spoon
> a skateboard
> a screen

The screen and the clothes rack are simple black silhouettes with operating rods attached.

You can make hangers easily by bending thin wire into the shape of coat hangers. Leave some without clothes for Scenes 2 and 4. Attach paper or fabric garments to the rest. Hang them on the rack just the way you would hang normal hangers, except that you need to bend the hook at the top at a right angle so that the hangers lie flat against the screen.

To get the size of the clothes and the rack correct, measure the Emperor puppet to find the size his clothes should be. Then make the rack to fit them.

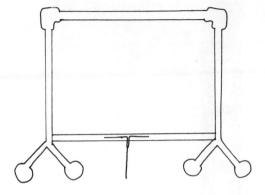

Illus. 92. Clothes rack.

Illus. 93. Screen: Attach the rod to the central upright of the frame.

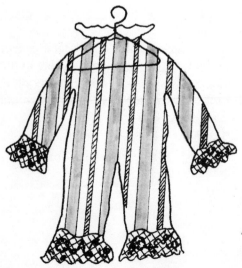

Illus. 94. One of the Emperor's old suits, made of striped paper and trimmed with pieces of black lace. Design the clothes to be funny or outrageous, using a variety of styles and materials.

116

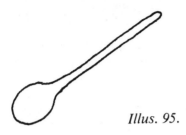

Illus. 95.

The spoon is also a simple silhouette which fits into a slit in the Queen's hand (the same way that the runcible spoon in "The Owl and the Pussy-Cat" fits into the cat's paw).

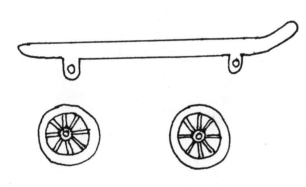

Illus. 96.

You need to exaggerate the design of the skateboard so that the audience can see it clearly. This will also increase the comic effect. Cut out the wheels and the board separately from the cardboard and then join them with a single strong thread, knotted on either side. Attach the Queen to it with a piece of plasticine. If you prefer, you could make the board from a double layer of cardboard and insert the Queen's feet between the layers.

For Scene 3, in the swindlers' attic, you need:

> a pair of scissors
> wine glasses
> a bottle

Cut out the two sections of the scissors separately and join them with a paper fastener or thread. Leave the connection loose enough to allow a "snipping" movement. Attach a rod to one section and fasten the other to the hand of the puppet with plasticine.

Illus. 97.

Cut the glasses and bottle out of paper and color them in. Rip-em holds one of the glasses. Attach it to his hand with plasticine. At the point that Rip-em gets rid of the glass, drop his arm to his side before pulling the glass away. Cut the other glass and the bottle as one piece, as though they were on a tray on the floor.

In Scene 5 the only new props you need are ropes to go around the necks of Rip-em and Puller. Pieces of string with a loop at one end will do very well. Make the loop large enough to slip over their heads easily.

The Puppets

On these pages you'll find some sample outlines for the puppets in the play. You may decide to design your own in an entirely different style. The whole play could be presented in an Eastern setting, for example.

As indicated here, the puppets are all made from white cardboard and colored with felt pens. The cardboard must be thick enough so that the puppets will lie flat against the screen, so choose your cardboard carefully, weighing its stiffness against its translucent qualities. Don't forget that when you oil the cardboard, you'll be making it more translucent.

More important than the appearance of the puppets is their ability to perform all the actions the play requires.

The Emperor

The Emperor has to walk, hold clothes up against himself and fall over when whacked by the Queen. Being a main character, he should be lively and able to react fully in every situation. You can also make joints at his knees for greater mobility, if you want. He should have a main rod for his body and rods on both hands.

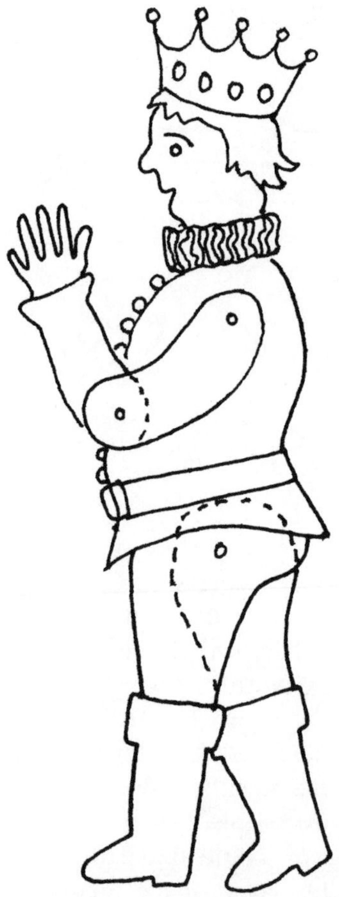

Illus. 98. Here is the Emperor joined at the elbows and shoulders. He has one moving leg. The puppet has another arm, identical to the one shown, attached to the other side of his body.

118

You need a second puppet – the Emperor without clothes – only for a short time. Here he has one jointed arm and a moving leg. The other arm is hidden by his body. More joints would help him react with more consternation when the crowd realizes he has no clothes on, but this is optional.

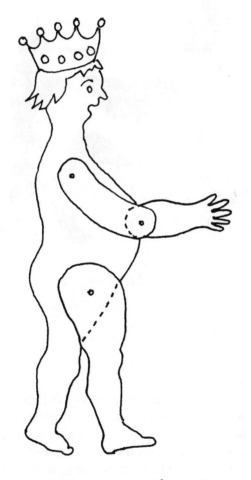

Illus. 99. Emperor – second puppet without clothes.

Illus. 100. Pressy.

Note: Pressy and the Queen also have a second arm on the other side of their bodies, identical to the ones shown.

Pressy

He needs to be fairly agile, particularly in his arms. He is jointed at the elbows and shoulders and has one moving leg. Like the Emperor, he needs three rods. With both these characters (and with the swindlers) you can hold an arm rod and body rod in one hand, as if they were one rod, for a great deal of the action. At other times, when the character is quiet, you can prop the body rod on the shelf while you manipulate the two wrist rods.

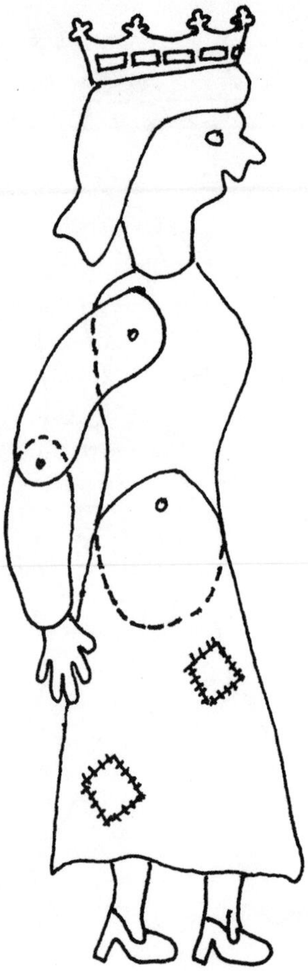

fancy outfit with lace and bows. If you want to follow this instruction, draw the outline of the dress a little larger than her basic dress, on tracing paper. Decorate it with a lacy pattern and bows (making sure that the bows cover the patches). Or you can use real lace, instead. Her basic dress color will show through as a background color. Attach the lace dress to her with transparent tape.

Illus. 101. Queen.

Illus. 102. Spot.

Queen

She is jointed at the waist and has one jointed arm. Her most complicated action is skateboarding. You can get her to wobble on the **skateboard** by moving her at the waist. One arm needs to be jointed so that she can wave her wooden spoon. If you want, when she changes her dress for Scene 4, you can make a new puppet, but this is not necessary.

The text indicates that she is wearing a

Spot

All Spot has to do is walk. Give him a single main body rod and two loosely jointed legs. You may want to add another rod to his front moving leg. This would give him a greater range of movement in Scene 3 when he is chased by the swindlers.

120

Rip-em and Puller

Both of these puppets are jointed at the elbow and shoulder and have one moving leg. Like the Emperor and Pressy, they have three rods and some complicated actions to perform. In Scene 3 they sit on the floor with their legs straight out in front of them. Puller also has to sit at the sewing machine, which he can do with stiff legs. However, you may decide to give the swindlers knee joints. This would enable them to kneel before the Emperor in the last scene. Your decision might depend on the skill of the puppeteers. A puppet with many joints can look wonderful in the hands of a skilled puppeteer, but with a less experienced operator, it may look as if it's doing terrible contortions.

Puller has to pick up the scissors. He can do it while he sits on the floor. Drop his arm to his side so it is screened by his body and attach the scissors to his hand.

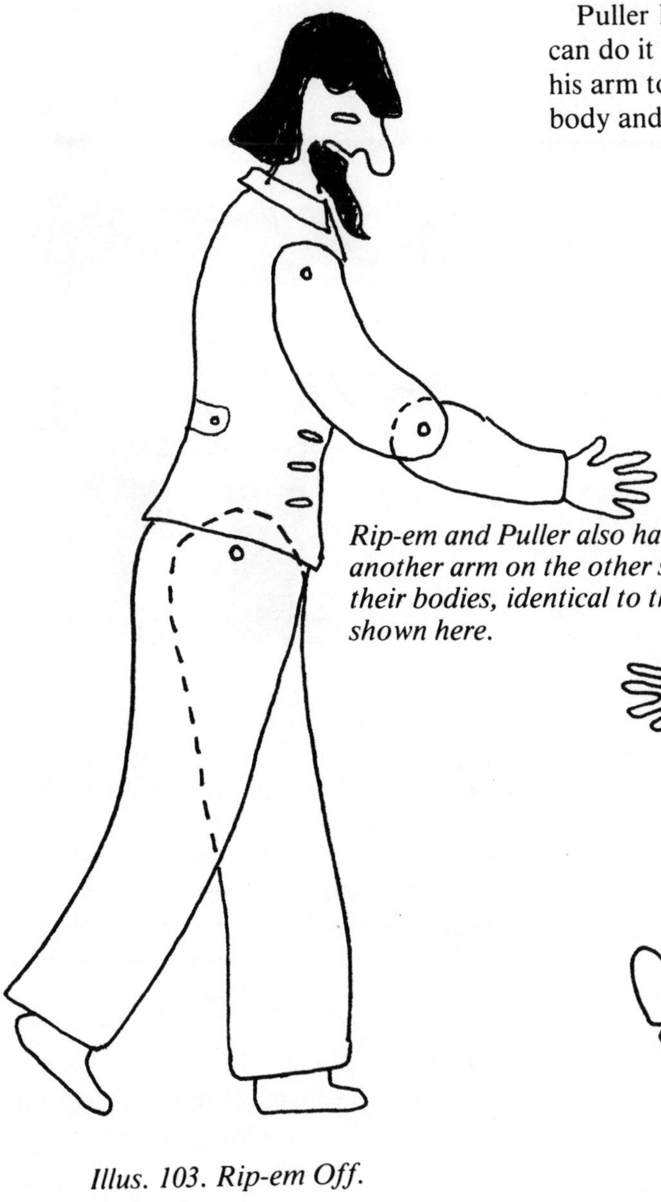

Rip-em and Puller also have another arm on the other side of their bodies, identical to the ones shown here.

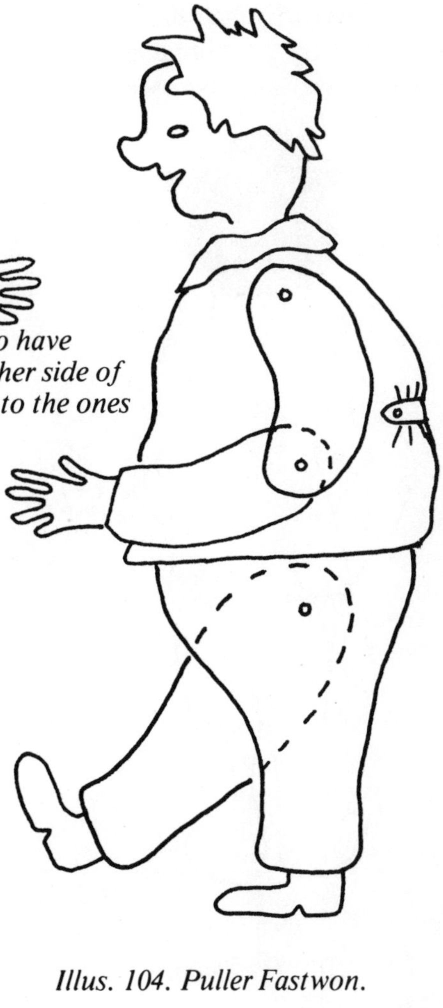

Illus. 103. Rip-em Off.

Illus. 104. Puller Fastwon.

To operate Puller with the scissors, hold the free arm rod, the body rod, and the scissors arm rod all in one hand. The scissors arm needs to stretch; you may have to bend the rod a little in order to do this. Your other hand is then free to operate the scissors rod. This is the most complicated action in the whole play; it requires practice. You need to get just the right degree of looseness in Puller's arm joint – and also in the thread or paper fastener joining the two sections of the scissors. Don't despair if it seems too difficult. It won't matter at all if you use a pair of scissors cut in one piece (in an open position) instead. Then all you have to do is to attach them to Puller's hand. You'll have the same situation when Rip-em uses the scissors at the end of the scene.

Illus. 106. The Town Crier.

Illus. 105. The Child.

Town Crier
This puppet has a small part, but two main actions. First he reads the proclamation. For this section, you could give him a bell, slipped into his hand, if you want. (Any small handbell will provide the sound effect offstage.) Second, he returns pulling the screen. He needs only one jointed limb for these movements – his arm.

The Child
His part, too, is small and he needs only one jointed arm. One finger should be extended in a pointing gesture.

The Crowd

Below you'll see The Crowd as a group puppet. Small holes are indicated for arm attachments. Five of these, each with an operating rod, enable the crowd to raise its arms when cheering.

Operating Rods

The main body rods of each puppet should be attached by a wire taped across the neck and emerging under the chin. This will allow them to face left or right without removing the rod. Color the puppets on one side only. Light will still shine through, even though the black side will sometimes be next to the screen. You'll need to bend the wire of the rod, so be careful to select a wire that is strong, but not too brittle.

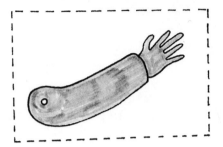

Illus. 108. Arm attachment.

Illus. 107. The Crowd.

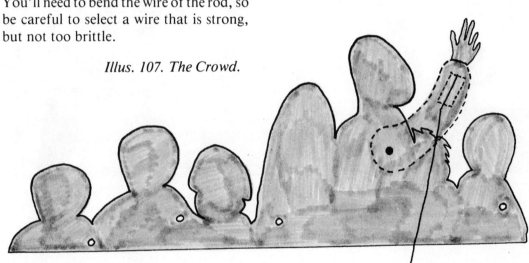

The practical suggestions for performing these plays have been given in some detail, but that is just to start you off. Draw your own puppets, work out your own scenery and props. Write your own dialogue – try the ideas given here for puppets and scenery and music in other plays that you adapt or originate yourself.

The shadow theatre is a very versatile medium, so set your imagination to work on the possibilities. You can achieve wonderful effects by the combination of good lighting, bold design and interesting textures. You have only to pick up a lifeless cardboard shape and see it transformed on the screen to know for yourself the magic of the shadow puppet theatre.

Illus. 109. Puppets from "The Emperor's New Clothes."

9. Shadow Puppets of the Past

No one knows for certain when shadow puppetry began. Originally, it appears to have been an Eastern art. It seems that shadow puppets have existed in China for over a thousand years. They were used to illustrate tales from Chinese history and stories about Buddha.

These early puppets were made of animal skins, beaten flat and oiled. This treatment made them so thin that the operating light could shine through the skin and reveal varying depths and shades. Sometimes the skins were delicately colored, giving an even richer effect. This was generally done after the figures had been cut to shape and patterned with intricate lace-like designs. These puppets were works of art, and carefully treasured by the puppeteers.

Some figures were particularly complex in design. An arm, for instance, might be jointed at shoulder, elbow and wrist. The puppeteers needed great skill to control the many jointed sections, which they manipulated with rods attached to the puppet's body and limbs. Although a puppet could have as many as a dozen different pieces, it would be controlled by only three rods, one attached to the neck of the figure and one to each hand, as you can see in the illustration of Hsia K'e on page 127.

The rods attached to the hands moved all three arm joints. The rod at the neck not only controlled the puppet's torso — so that it could bend at the waist, for instance — it also allowed the puppeteer to make the figure walk (aided by the fact that the puppet was held steady against the screen). This required just the right degree of tightness in the thread joining the separate pieces. If the thread was too loose, the limbs would just hang down. If it was too tight, the limbs wouldn't be able to move.

Any modern puppeteer can learn a great deal from studying these early Chinese puppets. Today few shadow puppets enthusiasts attempt to match their beauty and intricacy. For one thing, the modern puppeteers don't need to make such permanent figures as those owned by a travelling Chinese puppet company. The Chinese puppets needed to be particularly strong to withstand continuous repeated performances and the wear and tear of frequent packing and unpacking. But we can adapt some of the Chinese methods of jointing and rod control. On page 28 you'll find suggestions and ideas for creating puppets based on a Chinese model.

The Indonesian island of Java is another area that has a long history of shadow puppetry. In Java the teaching and stories of the Hindu religion provided the material for puppet plays. It was an important form of religious instruction.

These plays are performed even today. The puppeteers are more than entertainers; their role is close to that of a priest. These puppets too are treated with reverence.

Also popular in Java are the series of plays known as the Panji cycle. These are stories from the life of a legendary Javanese prince of the 10th century called "Panji."

Illustration 110 is typical of the stylized Javanese shadow puppets. As you can see, it is very different from the Chinese puppet, although the rods are attached to the head and wrists in similar ways.

The Javanese methods of preparing, cutting and coloring skins are also similar to those of the Chinese, but the design of the figures follows their own ancient, local traditions. With their ornate headdresses and long thin arms, Javanese shadow puppets are unlike those from any other countries. While they may have less to teach us in the way of design, we can still admire the tremendous care paid to the smallest detail. Some of the figures were richly decorated with gold leaf.

China and Java are just two of many places where shadow puppetry has had a long history. In Turkey, for instance, shadow puppets evolved in a very different direction, more like modern slapstick comedy than religious ceremony. A figure called "Karagoz" – a comic rascal who appeared in Turkish puppet plays in the 14th century – dominated the scene right up until the early 1900's. Television and films, it seems, have silenced this boisterous, lovable character as a popular form of entertainment, although he seems to have survived longer in Greece. Greek shadow traditions are entirely Turkish in origin.

Turkish puppets are less ornate than

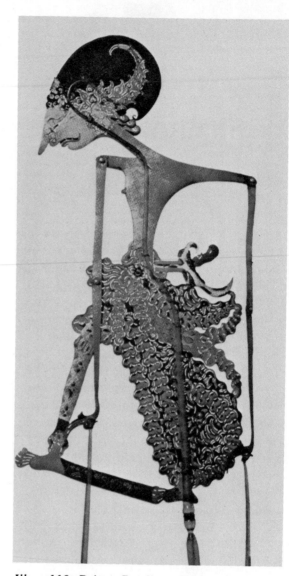

Illus. 110. Prince Panji – a Javanese shadow puppet.

Chinese and Javanese puppets. You don't find so much intricate cutting-out, although they use color wonderfully.

Many European countries have produced shadow puppets, and the art still thrives today. Moscow has a shadow theatre.

126

Illus. 111. Hsia K'e, Chinese shadow puppet from the Hetta Empson Collection.

Professional shadow performances can be seen occasionally in other countries, too, either at permanent puppet theatres or performed by travelling groups touring the country. Increasingly, there are shadow puppet exhibitions at museums with collections on display.

Another form of the art, developed in this century, is the shadow puppet film. The work of Lotte Reiniger, who lives in Britain but began her work in Germany, is outstanding in this field. Shadow puppet films are sometimes shown on television.

The craft of shadow puppetry, which has entertained men and women in different parts of the world for hundreds of years, can still provide much pleasure for people of all ages today. A shadow puppet can be as simple or as complex as you wish, but, whatever its design, it will be transformed magically when silhouetted against a brightly lit screen in a darkened room.

Index

128